One *Line* at a Time

24 Geometric Machine-Quilting
Designs Made Easy

C&T PUBLISHING

Text copyright © 2009 by Charlotte Warr Andersen

Artwork copyright © 2009 by C&T Publishing, Inc.

Publisher: Amy Marson

Creative Director: Gailen Runge

Editor: Liz Aneloski

Technical Editors: Sandy Peterson and Carol Zentgraf

Copyeditor/Proofreader: Wordfirm Inc.

Cover Designer/Book Designer: Kristy K. Zacharias

Page Layout Artist: Kerry Graham

Production Coordinator: Kirstie L. Pettersen

Illustrator: Tim Manibusan

Photography by Diane Pedersen and Christina Carty-Francis of C&T Publishing unless otherwise noted

Published by C&T Publishing, Inc., P.O. Box 1456, Lafayette, CA 94549

Library of Congress Cataloging-in-Publication Data

Andersen, Charlotte Warr,

One line at a time : 24 geometric machine-quilting designs made easy / Charlotte Warr Andersen.

p. cm.

Includes bibliographical references.

Summary: "Use simple tools to create elaborate geometric quilting fills without marking or only minimally marking the fabric. Includes a brief discussion of machine quilting, including thread, needles, and tension, and step-by-step instructions for quilting patterns with variations"--Provided by publisher.

ISBN 978-1-57120-531-5 (paper trade : alk. paper)

1. Patchwork--Patterns. 2. Machine quilting--Patterns. I. Title.

TT835.A49357 2009

746.46'041--dc22

2008026912

Printed in China

10 9 8 7 6 5 4 3

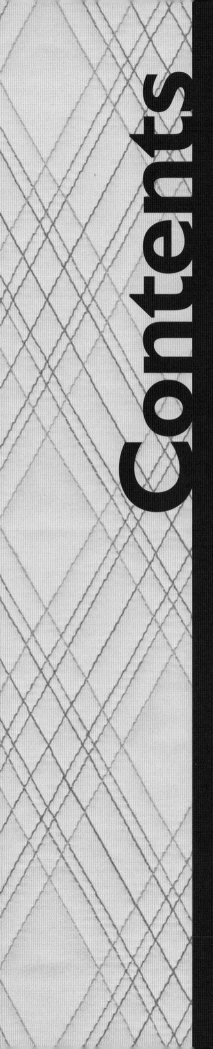

Contents

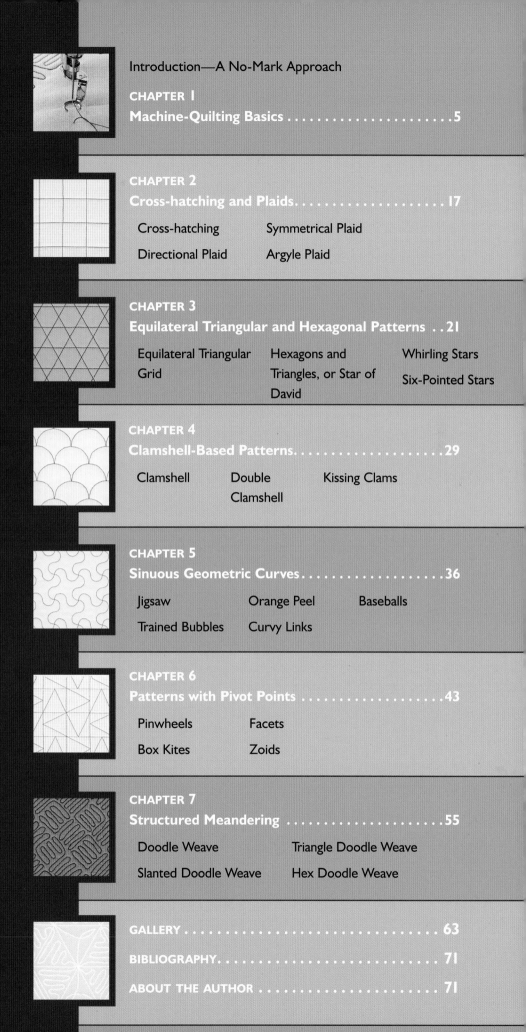

Introduction

A No-Mark Approach

How can you get precise geometric quilting patterns if you don't mark lines that can be followed with stitching?

Marking lines creates the problem of removing those lines after the quilting is done. The quilt usually must be laundered to remove the marks, and if the quilt cannot be laundered, the marks may remain.

A few years ago, I made a quilt containing mostly silk fabrics. I had not prewashed the silks, and several were in vibrant colors that I knew would run if I washed the quilt. I did not like the thought of having even subtle residues of marks left on the quilt. So I came up with a method of structuring precise geometric quilting patterns without having to mark with pencil, marker, or chalk on the actual quilt. My experience with that quilt became the basis for this book.

This book is intended for the machine quilter using a home sewing machine, although the patterns could easily be adapted for use by longarm machine quilters. As much as I admire the speed and perfection that can be achieved with longarm machines, especially the computerized ones, they're just not for me. I hope this book will help those of you who, like me, want to do quality quilting with your trusty home sewing machine.

Possibilities abound in the no-mark approach to machine quilting. Every pattern that I worked out in stages brought thoughts about new patterns or ways to elaborate on those I'd already formulated. My wish is that you take this book as a helpful tool for coming up with new and interesting ways to enrich the quilted surface.

Try playing with graph paper to see whether you can come up with your own designs. Remember, the goal is to make the design as continuous as possible, having as few starts and stops as possible. At http://incompetech.com/graphpaper/, you can print custom graph paper in many layouts: squares, hexagons, triangles, diamonds, circles, and so on, and you can specify the size of the shapes. I like to print large grids on the graph paper—it makes doodling easier.

Dedication

Having enjoyed (and, at times, endured) 35 years of marriage, I dedicate this book to my husband, Eskild, my soul mate. He is my biggest fan and greatest supporter. I need him every bit as much as he says he needs me, and I look forward to 35 more years with him, if we last that long.

Acknowledgments

My applause and esteem to the great quilters who have given us our rich heritage of machine work and who are always raising the bar: Harriet Hargrave, Debra Wagner, Caryl Bryer Fallert, and Diane Gaudynski, to name just a few. The originators and innovators are those who keep us in pursuit of excellence and help us push ourselves to come up with something new.

CHAPTER I

Machine-Quilting Basics

Test First

Many factors affect machine-quilting results. And these factors can change slightly from day to day, even if you use exactly the same equipment. Therefore, it is always wise to prepare a mini quilt sandwich (10″–12″ square) to test your machine quilting. Prepare this mini quilt using the fabrics and batting you plan to use in the project you are about to quilt. Stitch some test patterns. Then wash the mini quilt as you would the project quilt to make sure you're happy with your choices.

Batting

A low-loft (thin) batting is always preferable for machine quilting. High-loft (thick) batting is suitable only for tied quilts and is almost impossible to feed under the presser foot of a home sewing machine.

I have had success with several types of batting—cotton, wool, polyester, and blends. However, battings with identical fiber contents but made by different manufacturers may perform differently. I prefer to use batting made completely, or mostly, from natural fibers. It seems to cling to the quilt top and backing, so less slippage

occurs between the layers of the quilt sandwich during machine quilting.

Be sure to wash your mini quilt so you can see whether the batting will beard or not. Beards are little white fibers from the batting that poke through the fabric of the quilt top, and they may not appear until after laundering.

Basting the Quilt Sandwich

There are various ways to hold the top, batting, and backing layers together. Some quilters prefer to pin baste the quilt sandwich, but I find the pins too obtrusive and difficult to remove. I prefer to thread baste the quilt sandwich.

If the quilt is large, place it on the floor or a large table, or stretch it in a frame before quilting. If the quilt is small, place it on a table with a cutting mat under it to protect the tabletop. Use a 3″ soft-sculpture needle threaded with polyester cone thread (cheap stuff) and make 1″-long stitches in a crosshatch pattern of horizontal and vertical rows 3″–4″ apart. These rows of stitches don't have to be very straight; their only purpose is to hold the quilt layers together until an area is quilted.

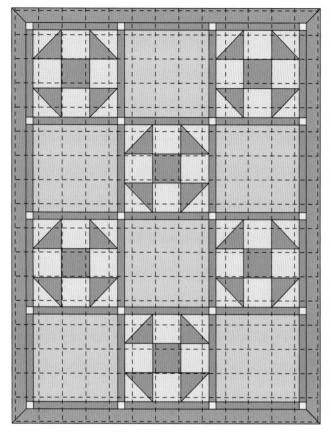

Hand basting a crosshatch grid

If the presser foot gets caught under one of the basting threads while you are machine quilting, just snip the thread. Once an area is quilted, pulling out the basting threads is easy, unless the quilting is very dense. If the quilting will be dense in an area, remove some of the basting thread from that area before you start quilting there.

You can also use adhesive spray (made especially for basting quilts) to hold your layers together. Be sure to use the spray outdoors.

You can also use fusible batting to hold the quilt sandwich together. Always test the batting first though (page 5). I used this kind of batting to make the small samples for this book, and the adhesive on one brand that I tried bled through to the surface of the fabric and made obvious stains. Mountain Mist fusible batting

worked acceptably well. Using fusible batting on large quilts can be a challenge. For this type of batting, use a large flat surface, such as a Formica tabletop, that can be ironed on safely with steam—definitely not a good wooden table. You can also pad the surface with towels or an old blanket.

Sewing Machines and Accessories

Your sewing machine must be in good working order: cleaned and oiled according to the directions in the user manual. If you haven't had the machine serviced in a long time, now might be the time to do so.

If you are shopping for a machine, take a sample quilt sandwich to the dealer so you can give your prospective machine a test drive. There are many lower-end machines that stitch well, so you don't necessarily have to spend a lot of money. Though not necessary, a needle-up/needle-down feature is a great aid in machine quilting.

For the techniques in this book, sewing machine accessories can be important.

SEWING MACHINE FEET

You must have a walking, or even-feed, foot. This foot allows the thickness of multiple layers to be fed under the foot without shifting and is vital when you are stitching straight lines.

Most machines have a walking foot that either comes with the machine or can be purchased as an extra. Determine your walking foot's measurements so you can use it to plan the spacing of your stitching lines. On the Bernina walking foot, for example, the distance from the centered needle to both outside edges of the foot is ½″, so if you place an outside edge of the foot on a line of previous stitching, you will get ½″ between stitching lines. If you look carefully, you will notice that you can use other edges of the foot as guides to create several different spacings between your lines of stitching. Additionally, if your machine's needle position can be adjusted to the left or right, you can obtain a multitude of finely calibrated widths within the range of the foot.

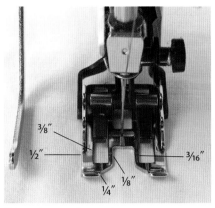

Edges that can be used as measurement guides on a walking foot

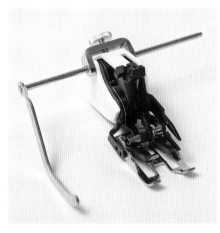

Bernina walking foot with seam guide

You will also need a presser foot suitable for free-motion quilting. I prefer the Bernina freehand embroidery foot (no. 24), which, in my opinion, provides the most visibility for machine quilting.

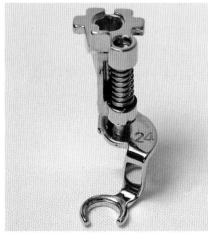

Bernina freehand embroidery foot (no. 24)

SEAM GUIDES

If you want to stitch lines that are farther apart than the spacings you can achieve with the edges of the presser foot, you will need a seam guide that attaches to the presser foot or sewing machine. The measurements on the stitch plate are hidden once the quilt is on top of it, so they can't help you in the quilting process. The leg of the seam guide rides on the surface of the quilt, and the distance from the needle to the leg is adjustable, so you can use it as a guide to sew an exact distance. Some machines come with both right and left seam guides. I like the one that attaches to the left side of the foot because that is where I try to keep the bulk of my quilt. A seam guide can be used with feet other than the walking foot, and you can experiment with these feet to see whether you can get desirable results. However, the walking foot will do the best job of keeping the quilt flat.

How to Use a Seam Guide

Determine the spacing needed between the quilting lines. If close cross-hatching is desired, various "edges" on the walking foot (above) can be used as a guide from the starter lines. Use a starter line as a guide. A starter line can be an existing stitching line, a scored line (page 17), a taped line, a fabric edge, and so on. If wider crosshatching is desired, use a seam guide. With the walking foot on the machine and the seam guide attached, place a ruler under the foot with one of the ruler's inch marks right under the needle. Slide the leg of the seam guide to the desired spacing between quilting lines (for example, 1½″) and tighten the seam guide in place. The leg will ride on top of your starter line as you stitch quilting lines. As you progress, the leg will ride on a previously completed quilting line.

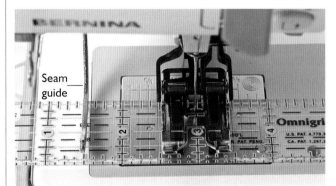

Walking foot with seam guide and ruler

After you tighten the screw on the seam guide, recheck the distance between the leg of the guide and the needle because it may have shifted a little. Be sure to sight off one side of the seam guide consistently, because the guide is about ⅛″ wide.

Needles

Use a needle that is designated for quilting in a size to match the type of thread you're using.

If you plan to quilt with metallic thread, you will need to use a topstitching needle or a needle for metallic thread to get good stitches with little thread breakage.

Threads

Many types of thread are available for machine quilting, and which type to use is a matter of preference. There are thick threads that have a visible impact on the quilt, variegated threads that create subtle movement for the eye, metallics that add a lovely sparkle, and fine machine-embroidery threads that create delicate lines. The most important element is that the thread is good quality, so that it doesn't break frequently. There is nothing more frustrating than a thread that constantly snaps.

Truthfully, you can use just about any thread for machine quilting. Some threads are going to work better than others, and you usually get what you pay for: inexpensive thread does not always perform well. Be sure to test your thread first.

Machine-quilting threads

Thread does not have to have the words "machine quilting" on the spool end or on the packaging to be used for machine quilting. Although you can use hand-quilting thread in a machine, it does not always feed well or give the best-looking stitch. I have also found some threads labeled for machine quilting that were awful in my machine.

I've also had friends recommend a thread for machine quilting that they said worked wonderfully in their machines and looked great on their quilts. However, that same thread performed abysmally in both my machines (whose names are Augustina and Yulia, by the way). So I just have to say again that you should try a thread to see how it works for you.

For the most part, I prefer cotton threads. They perform best in my machines and seem to play well with the fabrics I have used. I have also used polyester threads with great success. I like the look of rayon and have had favorable results with it; but it is a bit slippery, and I worry about knots coming loose. For a truly impressive look, I adore metallic threads. Most of the quilting on *Starcrossed* (page 16) was done with Superior brand metallic thread. I had only a miniscule amount of breakage, which is extraordinary for metallic thread, and quilting with it was an amazing experience.

Most of the time I use the same thread in the bobbin and in the top when I quilt. Even though both my machines are quality ladies and great performers, and even though I think I have the tension well adjusted on them, every once in a while they will throw a less-than-desirable stitch. If I'm using the same thread in both bobbin and needle, the imperfect stitch is usually not a problem.

Thread Tension

Ideally, when you are machine quilting, the thread tension should be balanced so that there is an even amount of each thread on each side of the quilt. Loops of bobbin thread that come through to the front of the quilt, and loops of needle thread that peak through on the back of the quilt, are unattractive. You can achieve balance by working with either the tension control for the top thread or the tension screw on the bobbin. Refer to your sewing machine manual for instructions on adjusting thread tension. Work with the top thread tension control first to see whether you can get a desirable balance. Working with the tension screw on the bobbin is a bit more delicate.

Stitch Length

The stitch length you choose largely depends on the desired finished look of the quilt. Tiny stitches don't look attractive when done in a heavy thread. The finer the thread that I am using for quilting, the smaller I make my stitch length. Most of the time when using a walking foot, I use the default stitch length (usually 2.5) on my machine. However, if the quilt is small in scale and I'm using embroidery thread for quilting, I will decrease the stitch length. Some of the patterns in this book are so angularly geometric that you can count the number of stitches between corners. In this case, you can adjust the stitch length to fit.

Machine-Quilting Aids

There are many products on the market designed to help with machine quilting.

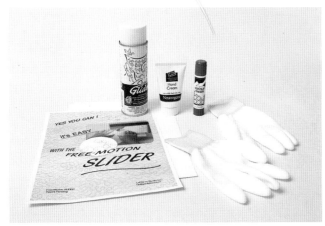

Machine-quilting aids

I have tried several products to improve my grip on my quilt as I stitch: Clover Non-Slip Finger, a glue-stick-like dispenser that you apply to your fingertips; Neutrogena hand cream, which makes your hands slightly tacky; and Machingers gloves.

As for the sewing machine surface, there are at least two kinds of silicone sheets that you can apply to the table of the sewing machine to help the quilt to glide somewhat more easily. There is also an aerosol product called Quilt Glide that you can spray on the surface of the machine table.

The purchase that helped me the most with my machine quilting was a sewing machine cabinet with a large, level surface that can support most, if not all, of a quilt. Having to pull the quilt up and over the edges of a small quilting surface creates a lot of drag—both on your quilting lines (causing inaccuracies) and your shoulders.

Continuous Lines

The fewer starts and stops you make when machine quilting (page 14), the less work you'll have tidying up the loose thread ends. This is why continuous quilting lines are desirable. Some quilting patterns are naturally continuous, whereas some have to be modified to make them continuous. Continuity can be created by backtracking, or stitching over previously stitched lines (overstitching). However, overstitching can look heavy if thread builds up or if the stitching over previous threads is inaccurate. It all depends on the look you desire. If I feel that an accumulation of thread will be distracting on my finished quilt, I am perfectly willing to do the extra finishing work caused by more starts and stops.

If you can begin or end a stitching line on the edge of a quilt, no knots are needed—the thread ends will be encased in the binding.

To make stitching continuous lines more successful, practice. The easiest way to try out the patterns in this book is to make several 10″–12″-square quilt sandwiches. Most of the patterns fit well into a square this size, and you can stitch from one edge to the other without worrying about burying threads. (If worked on slightly larger quilt sandwiches, they could be used for placemats.) Practice the patterns on these samples first because when you are working on a larger piece, doing the pivots and turns that are needed is much more challenging. When working on an important piece, you will want to concentrate on precision rather than on the mechanics of how the pattern is stitched, so practice first.

Pattern Templates

For many of the quilting designs in this book, you will need to make a pattern template on a full-sheet sticky label with a peel-off backing. These labels are available at your local office supply store and can be used over and over until they lose their stickiness.

> **Note:** The least expensive place I have found to purchase these labels in bulk is OnlineLabels.com, where you can get them in packages of 100 sheets.

The labels are 8½″ × 11″, so your pattern template is limited to 11″. If you need a longer template, you can cut out several designs and stick them together, aligning the shapes, to form a long template. However, an easier method involves what I call "leapfrogging." If you come to the end of a template and you need to do more stitching beyond the end of the template, leave the needle down in the fabric at a red arrow, raise the presser foot, carefully peel up the template, and move it forward, aligning the red arrows. Lower the presser foot and continue stitching.

The backing paper on the labels has seams to make it easy to remove. Many times, after you cut out a template, there won't be a seam on the back. Make your own seam using the sharp point of a pin to lightly score the backing paper—be careful not to go all the way through to the sticky label. Then bend the label at the score line and peel off the backing.

Sometimes, when you're working at the edge of a quilt, the template may hang over the edge. Take care to keep the template from sticking to the surface of the table.

Depending on the presser foot you are using, the edge of the foot may go under the sticky template and cause problems. If this happens, stop with the needle down in the fabric and lift the presser foot so it is on top of the template. Make sure the template is stuck back down firmly in that area.

I'm comfortable using the adhesive on these templates with my quilts. I have used the templates on silk with no harmful effects that I can see. However, I would advise that you not leave the templates on the fabric for long periods, as doing so would give the adhesive more time to sink into the fabric.

Using Tape to Mark the Design

You can use pre-marked Inchie Ruler Tape (available from C&T Publishing) or hand mark masking tape to create your quilting designs.

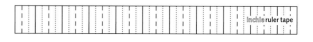

If using masking tape, make sure it is the exact width you need or your divisions will not be exact and square. Some brands are a little narrower than the measurement stated on the package. You can see the slight difference between the two types of 1″ tapes below.

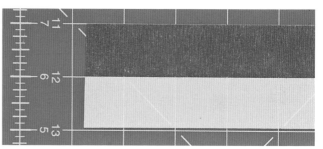

The blue tape is 1″ wide; the ecru tape is $^{15}/_{16}$″ wide.

Where Geometry and Free Forms Entwine

Once a quilt top has been completed, the next decision involves how to quilt it—which patterns to use, the scale of those patterns, and how to make them enhance the design of the top while being an integral part of the quilt.

The scale of the quilting patterns can have great impact both visually and physically on a quilt. Because of the amount of work involved, a small-scale pattern is going to be a lot more impressive than one done with lots of space between quilting lines.

All the designs in this book are scalable—you just need to be able to do simple math to reduce or enlarge them. For instance, if you wanted to make the Clamshell pattern (page 29) at half size, use a photocopy machine to reduce the template by 50%. If you want to make the Six-Pointed Stars pattern (page 26) smaller, reduce the triangular grid size to 1″ and copy the template at a 50% reduction.

COMPLETING INTERRUPTED LINES

When quilting lines intersect appliqué shapes, oftentimes the lines get interrupted, and determining how to complete the pattern can be a challenge, especially since we're trying to refrain from marking the quilt. As I come to these shapes, I try to visualize what the fragmented edges of the pattern look like and finish the lines accordingly. These fragments might not always be quite true to the geometry of the pattern when I follow through with my stitches.

If you need perfect lines, it may help to make an overlay of the pattern. Draw a repeat or two of the pattern to scale on a piece of write-on transparency film or some see-through vinyl. C&T Publishing makes a great product called Quilter's Vinyl for this application. Place the overlay on top of the quilt where the quilting pattern gets interrupted, and you will see where the interrupted lines need to be completed.

Pattern overlay for fragments

As a quilting line comes to the outline of an appliqué shape, you can end the line there; or, for continuity's sake, you can choose to stitch around the outline of the shape to where the next line of the quilting pattern may be picked up (traveling).

I have done it both ways. In *Starcrossed* (page 16), I ended all the lines of gold metallic quilting thread as they came to the edge of the black piping. Traveling along the edge of the piping to the next quilting line would have made the quilting easier, but I didn't want the heavy gold thread outlining the piping. I buried all the ends of those gold threads in the plaid.

Detail of plaid quilting on *Starcrossed*

In *Anodyne* (page 63), I traveled the stitching along the borders and around the embroidered figure of the woman. I was using a contrasting thread, but I decided that the extra contrast added by the outline of ecru next to the black would make the figure pop a bit more.

Detail of quilting on *Anodyne*

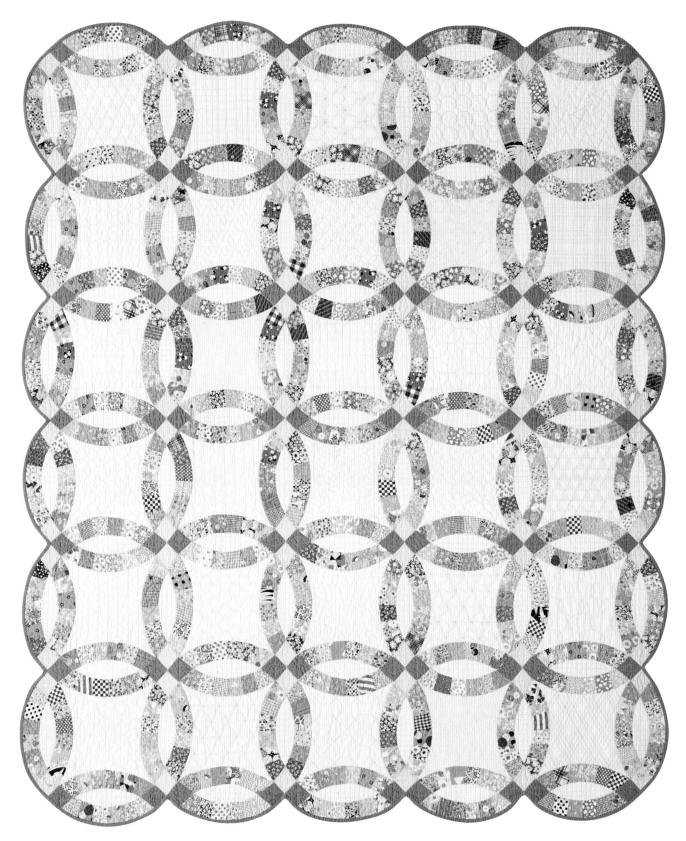

Double Charlotte, pieced by Charlotte Lee Warr, quilted by Charlotte Warr Andersen

BUTTING PATTERNS

Mixing quilting patterns is possible; I have never heard of a rule that says a background can be quilted in only one pattern. You may be able to make some of these patterns transition smoothly from one into another, particularly if they have the same grid measurement—patterns with equilateral triangular grids come particularly to mind. However, if you have a mix of patterns and scales that do not transition perfectly, you should have some sort of division between them. It can be as simple as a single stitched line. In *Starcrossed* (page 16), the patterns are separated either by piping or a heavy satin stitch. My grandmother's Double Wedding Ring quilt top (page 12) became a sampler of the quilting patterns in this book, and they were separated by the patchwork of the rings.

Compaction

"Compaction" is my term for what happens to a quilt sandwich when it is quilted. My friend Georgia Bonesteel calls it "take up." The more quilting stitches you put in a quilt, the more it tends to shrink up (compact). When dense quilting surrounds an unquilted area, the unquilted area tends to puff up and look almost like trapunto. Mixing different quilting patterns may cause the quilting to look uneven, especially if the patterns are quite different in scale or density. If the number of quilting stitches in two adjacent 3″ squares is drastically different, the result may look uneven. However, every one of the patterns

on my grandmother's Double Wedding Ring quilt (page 12) is in the size directed in this book, and the quilt lies flat. I think the mixture of quilting patterns worked because the bands of the rings are all quilted in the same manner, and they frame and separate each pattern nicely.

There is no mathematical equation to determine how much a quilt will compact. I tend to judge by eye, observing how many lines are in a pattern, how close together they are, and whether overstitching is involved.

Why is compaction important? If a quilt is to lie flat, it should have a relatively consistent density of quilting over the whole surface. Most of my quilts are not quite flat when I am finished with them. I launder most of them in the washer and dryer (just until slightly damp) after they are finished. If a quilt is still not flat after being washed, I iron it. *Starcrossed* (page 16) could not be laundered, because of the delicate fabrics in it, but I ironed it using steam to get it to lie as flat as possible, so that it hangs well.

Density of Quilting

Heavy/dense quilting is impressive. Many prize-winning quilts look as though they couldn't have another stitch put on them because they have been quilted so heavily. Not all quilts need to be quilted like that. Even a quilt that is going to be used frequently may not need closely packed quilting. Spaces can be left open, but open spaces should serve a design purpose. Spaces should not be left unquilted just because the minimum density required by the batting has been reached or because coming up with quilting for a certain space is too much work. I've seen many quilts in which the blocks were well quilted, but the 2″ or 3″ sashing between the blocks was left unquilted. This results in an unfinished look—adding quilting lines ¼″ away from the sashing seams results in a much more finished look.

Sometimes in my art quilts, there are areas where I do not want a lot of quilting, because I want to allow the batting to puff out a bit or because additional lines of quilting could actually distract from the look I want to achieve.

In the end, where to quilt and where not to quilt is your choice. You're the one who needs to be pleased with what you have created.

Finishing

STARTING AND STOPPING THE STITCHING

Option 1

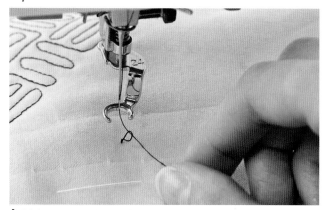

1. Make your needle go down through the quilt and up again once. Tug on the top thread, and a loop of the bobbin thread will appear.

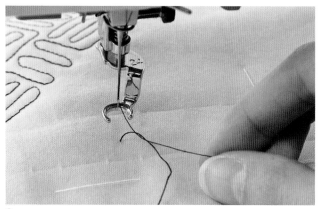

2. Pull the end of the bobbin thread all the way to the top.

Option 2

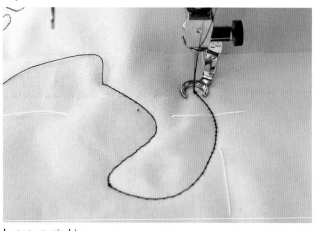

Just start stitching.

Note: If I use Option 1, I can pull up the bobbin thread only when the needle is up, and the quilt may move as I pull. Then I have to re-center the needle over that spot again. Therefore, I prefer to start my stitching using Option 2. Sometimes I end up with thread tangles on the back when I stitch many rows and the bobbin thread gets caught up in the later rows. Somehow, dealing with tangles seems easier to me than pulling the bobbin thread to the top.

DEALING WITH THREAD ENDS

If you begin or end the stitching on the edge of a quilt, no knots are needed—the thread ends will be encased in the binding.

Easy-threading needle

There are numerous methods for starting and ending the stitching in the middle of the quilt, but I prefer to tie knots—lots and lots of knots. It's kind of tedious work (I do it in front of the television), but the beautifully finished ends are worth it. My favorite tool for tying knots is a self-threading, or easy-threading, needle. This inexpensive needle has two eyes in the end. The lower one is like the eye of a regular needle that you have to poke the end of the thread through, but the upper eye has an opening in it between the two crests at the top. You can pull the side of the thread through this opening, and the upper eye is shaped so that the thread does not pop back out through the opening.

Even within a package, some of these needles work better than others. Some will cut the thread rather than let it pop into the eye—throw these away. There will be others in the package that work fine.

To deal with thread ends, use the following method.

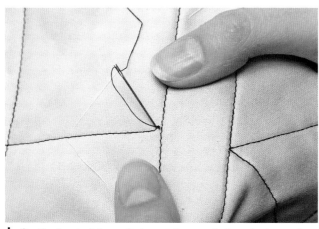 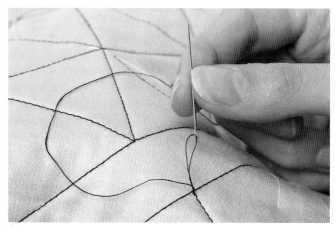

1. On the front of the quilt, insert the needle into the base of the 1ˢᵗ (or last) stitch through the quilt and pop the thread into the needle. Leave a loop of thread. If the thread is pulled up tightly against the needle, it may pop out of the eye before it is pulled through.

2. Bring the top thread through to the back of the quilt.

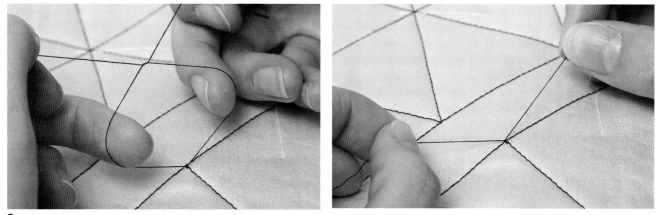

3. With both threads on the back of the quilt, tie a square knot (right over left, then left over right, or vice versa) close to the fabric.

  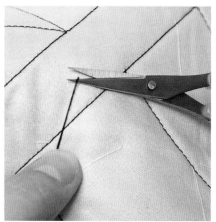

4. Pop both thread ends into the needle. Insert the needle into the backing of the quilt and then pull it out at least 1″ away.

5. Pull the needle through the backing, grab the threads, and give them a slight tug to pop the knot through the backing and into the batting.

6. Snip the remainder of the thread ends off at the surface of the quilt.

BINDING THAT ENHANCES

I used to think that a bias binding was the way to go, but lately I've been making straight-grain binding, which also works perfectly well. I've heard that certain members of the "quilt police" believe that all bindings should be ¼" wide. I think a binding can be wider than that as long as it enhances, rather than draws attention from, the quilt as a whole.

Starcrossed (below) has a binding that really does a lot for the quilt. The ½"-wide binding is made out of a striped silk fabric and has a lot of the same colors as the quilt top.

I also think of a binding as a way to "frame" my quilt. Whereas a line going off the edge of a quilt tends to keep the eye traveling, a narrow edge of binding, along with borders, helps to contain the eye to the interior of the quilt.

Starcrossed by Charlotte Warr Andersen

CHAPTER 2

Cross-hatching and Plaids

Cross-hatching

Cross-hatching (also known as grid work) consists of sets of parallel stitched lines that cross either at 90° to create squares or rectangles or at 60° to create diamonds. A quilting design based on cross-hatching a simple 90° grid is described below.

> *Note:* Another option for marking the baselines is to place a strip of masking tape next to the edge of a ruler or yardstick and then stitch along the edge of the tape.

1. To make the 90° base lines, start at the center of the area to be quilted and use a dull tapestry needle (or a Hera Marker) and a ruler to score a vertical line on the surface of the fabric from one edge of your quilt area to the other. Then score a horizontal line, also in the center. These are the only lines that need to be marked.

2. Stitch on the baselines.

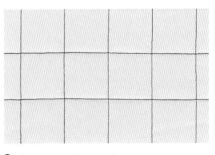

3. Determine the spacing you want between the subsequent lines of stitching. Use the edges of the walking foot (page 6) or adjust the seam guide (page 7) to achieve the proper spacing. Working outwards on both sides of the base lines, stitch parallel lines until the space has been filled, making a grid.

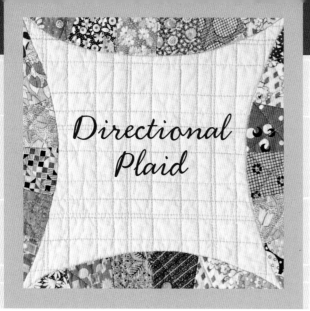

Directional Plaid

Quilting designs based on plaids, that is, irregularly spaced rows of cross-hatching, can be much more interesting than designs based on simple cross-hatching, especially if the stitching is done with many colors of thread or with variegated thread.

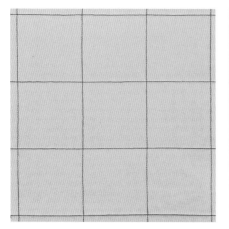

1. Score 90° baselines (page 17). Then set the seam guide on your walking foot at 3″ (page 7) and fill the desired area with 3″-wide cross-hatching, as shown in purple stitching.

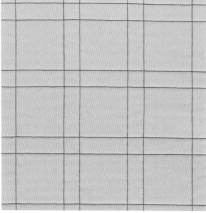

2. Set the seam guide at ³/₄″ and stitch on the right side of each of the baselines, as shown in red stitching.

3. Use an edge of the walking foot to give you ³/₁₆″ spacing (page 6) and stitch to the right of the red lines, as shown in green stitching.

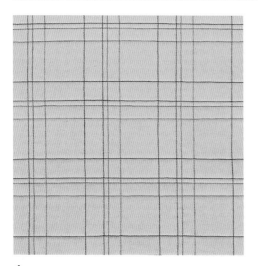

4. Use an edge of the walking foot to give you ¹/₂″ spacing and stitch to the right of the green lines, as shown in orange stitching.

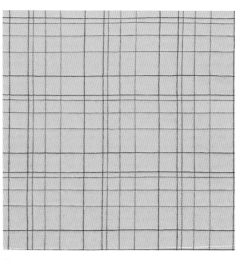

5. Set the seam guide at ⁵/₈″ and stitch to the right of the orange lines, as shown in blue stitching.

Symmetrical Plaid

If you desire balance and symmetry, try the Symmetrical Plaid pattern. The resulting pattern makes a lively and exciting background filler. Once you understand the principles of creating these straight-line patterns, you can create your own designs. The distances between the stitching lines may be changed as desired to create an infinite number of plaids—just remember to keep a consistent structure.

1. Score 90° baselines (page 17).

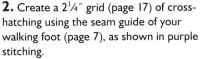

2. Create a 2¼″ grid (page 17) of cross-hatching using the seam guide of your walking foot (page 7), as shown in purple stitching.

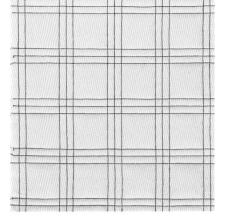

3. Use an edge of the walking foot to give you ⁵⁄₁₆″ spacing (page 6) and stitch on both sides of the baselines, as shown in red stitching.

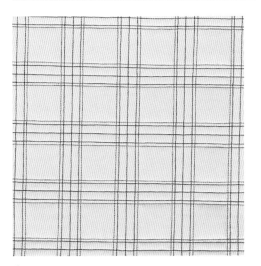

4. Use an edge of the walking foot to give you ⅛″ spacing and stitch outside each of the red lines, as shown in green stitching.

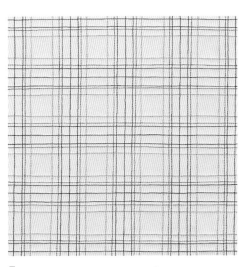

5. Use an edge of the walking foot to give you ¼″ spacing and stitch outside of each of the green lines, as shown in orange stitching.

Argyle Plaid

The Symmetrical Plaid (page 19) can also be turned into an argyle pattern using a rotary cutting ruler and the 60° line.

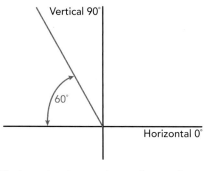

Horizontal and vertical score lines and the first 60° score line

1. Score 90° baselines (page 17). These lines will not be stitched. Place the ruler's 60° angle line on the horizontal score line and score the 60° angle line to mark the first starter line. Extend this line by moving the ruler below the horizontal score line if necessary.

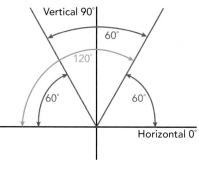

Opposing 60° line

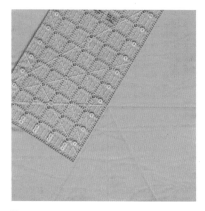

2. Flip the ruler over and position it to create an opposing 60° line. Score the line. Extend the line by moving the ruler below the horizontal score line if necessary.

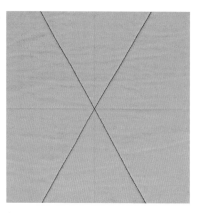

3. Stitch the two 60° starter lines.

4. Using the 60° starter lines, create a diamond-based grid using the measurements described for the Symmetrical Plaid (page 19).

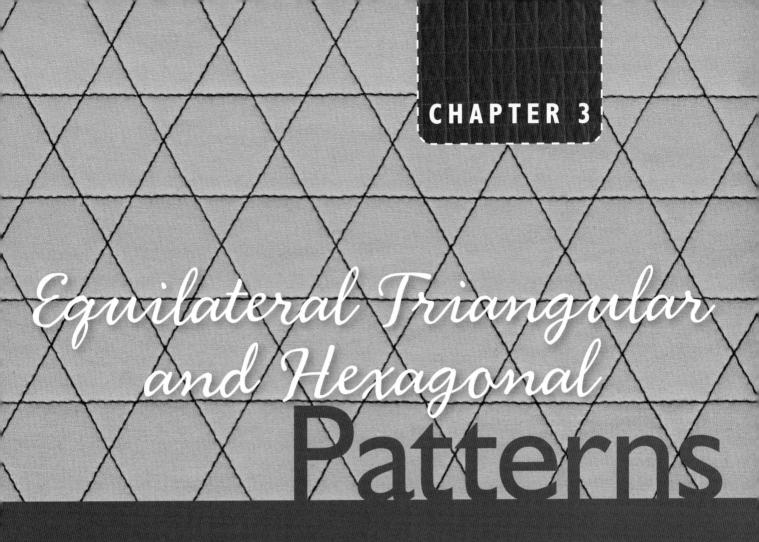

CHAPTER 3

Equilateral Triangular and Hexagonal Patterns

An equilateral triangle is something you most likely learned about in math class sometime during your educational career. For quilting purposes, all you need to remember is that an equilateral triangle has three equal sides and three 60° angles. If six equilateral triangles are grouped around a common center, then a hexagon is formed.

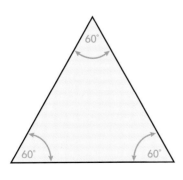

Equilateral triangle

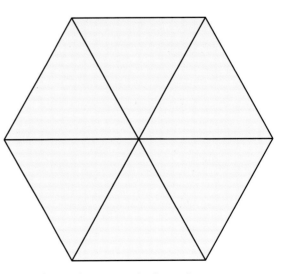

Six equilateral triangles form a hexagon

Equilateral Triangular Grid

M any hexagonal quilting patterns are based on equilateral triangles. Let's start with a simple design using equilateral triangles.

Plan how the triangles will best fit into the area you want to quilt. If you have a long straight line on the edge of the area, make that your base line and then fill the entire space with parallel lines. If the space has no straight lines, you might simply want to score a horizontal line through the middle of the area and build outward from both sides of this line.

1. Score a baseline (page 17) and stitch on that line. Set the seam guide of your walking foot at 1″ (page 7) and stitch a set of parallel lines.

2. Place the ruler's 60° line (page 20) on one of the 1st set of stitched lines and score a line along the edge of the ruler using a dull tapestry needle.

3. Using the score line and the seam guide of your walking foot set at 1″, stitch a 2nd set of parallel lines over the 1st. Fill the space.

Note: It is easy to keep the third set of lines looking straight when stitching from intersection to intersection when you are doing large-scale quilting patterns. When you do small-scale patterns, such as in *Anodyne* (page 63), the intersections may not line up correctly, and inaccuracies may be more apparent. These inaccuracies will show up more readily if the only quilting pattern used is the triangles. However, if additional lines are added over the grid, then the inaccuracies (crooked lines) aren't so noticeable.

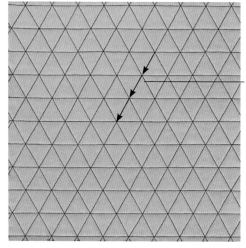

Stitch from 1 intersection to the next.

4. Stitch a straight line from one intersection to the next intersection across the diamonds that have been formed. Fill the space. You can use the seam guide, but the important thing is to be sure that the new lines of stitching go right through the centers of the previously stitched intersections. When the needle is down at one intersection, point your presser foot at the next intersection and stitch a straight line to it. Fill the space.

Hexagons and Triangles, or Star of David

The Hexagons and Triangles pattern is a bit more exciting than using allover triangles, and it creates a pleasing background fill. This pattern is stitched using the same steps as the Equilateral Triangular Grid (page 22) for the first two sets of parallel lines.

1. Score a baseline (page 17) and stitch on that line. Set the seam guide of your walking foot at 1″ (page 7) and stitch a set of parallel lines.

2. Place the ruler's 60° line (page 20) on one of the 1st set of stitched lines and score a line along the edge of the ruler using a dull tapestry needle. Using the score line and the seam guide of your walking foot set at 1″, stitch a 2nd set of parallel lines over the 1st. Fill the space.

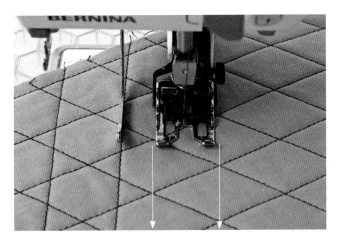

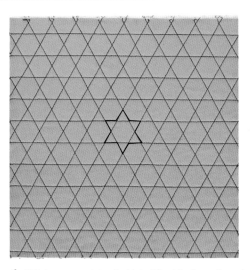

3. For the 3rd set of parallel lines, sight both outside edges of the walking foot on imaginary lines connecting the intersections of the first 2 sets of parallel lines, and set the seam guide between the 2 sets of intersections. Stitch the 3rd set of parallel lines. If you do not use a Bernina foot, then adapt measurements on your walking foot or the seam guide to create this set of quilting lines.

4. Fill the area with stitching. The black outline shows the Star of David

Whirling Stars

The Whirling Stars design is based on a 1½″ grid of equilateral triangles (page 21) with undulating lines stitched over the top of the grid. This design requires some structured free-motion stitching. Free-motion stitching involves moving the quilt with your hands while the needle is going up and down. The feed dogs need to be dropped so that the machine is no longer controlling the flow of fabric

1. Score a line (page 17) and stitch on that line. Set the seam guide of your walking foot at 1½″ (page 7) and stitch a set of parallel lines.

2. Place the ruler's 60° line (page 20) on one of the 1st set of stitched lines and score a line along the edge of the ruler using a dull tapestry needle. Using the score line and the seam guide set at 1½″, stitch a 2nd set of parallel lines over the 1st. Fill the space.

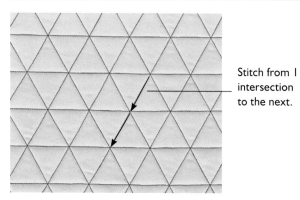

Stitch from 1 intersection to the next.

3. Stitch a straight line from one intersection to the next intersection. You can use the seam guide, but the important thing is to be sure that the new lines of stitching go right through the centers of the previously stitched intersections. When the needle is down at one intersection, point your presser foot at the next intersection and stitch a straight line to it. Fill the space.

Note: If you have a Bernina, here is a great opportunity to try out the Bernina Stitch Regulator, which will give evenly spaced stitches. Many quilters who have had trouble getting the hang of free-motion stitching have had success with this device.

under the needle—you are. Many quilters think that they need to stitch fast when doing free-motion quilting. I find that the opposite is true. I would rather go slowly so I can regulate the length of my stitches more easily and consistently. I use a Bernina freehand embroidery foot (no. 24; page 7).

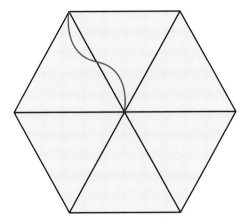

4. Change to your preferred presser foot for free-motion stitching. If your machine has a needle-up/needle-down feature, select the needle-down option. Starting at one corner of a triangle, stitch an S curve over one side of the triangle.

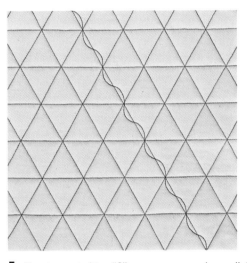

5. Continue stitching "S" curves over each parallel line, from intersection to intersection, as shown in red stitching. Stitch the curves over each of the 3 sets of parallel lines.

Note: You can also stitch "Z" curves; see Six-Pointed Stars (page 26). For both the "S" curve and the "Z" curve, you must place the curves consistently to create the "whirling" effect. If you mix the curves, the design will not have the desired symmetry.

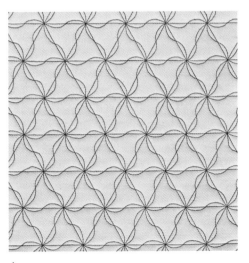

6. Continue to fill the area.

Six-Pointed Stars

The Six-Pointed Stars pattern is one of the most recognizable Sashiko (Japanese stitching) patterns, and it looks complicated. However, by breaking it down into components, you can easily stitch it with no marking.

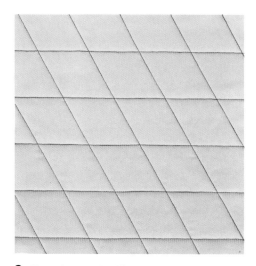

1. Score a horizontal line using a dull tapestry needle and a ruler (page 17). Stitch on this line. Stitch parallel lines, 2″ apart, using the seam guide (page 7). Check the spacing after you stitch the 2nd parallel line; the lines must be exactly 2″ apart for the star design to work.

2. Place the ruler's 60° line (page 20) on one of the 1st set of stitched lines and score a line along the edge of the ruler using a dull tapestry needle. Using the score line and the seam guide set at 2″, stitch a 2nd set of parallel lines over the 1st. Fill the space.

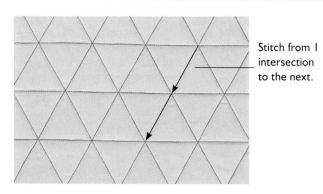

Stitch from 1 intersection to the next.

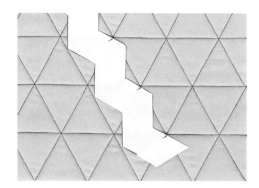

3. Stitch a straight line from one intersection to the next intersection, creating equilateral triangles (page 21). Fill the space. You can still use the seam guide, but it is more important to be sure the new line of stitching goes right through the center of the previously stitched intersections. When the needle is down at 1 intersection, point your presser foot at the intersection at the closest opposite corner and sew a straight line to it.

4. Copy the template pattern (page 28) on sticky label paper and cut on the zigzag lines. Peel off the paper backing. Position the template along one of the straight lines, so the red arrows on the template match up to the intersections of the triangles.

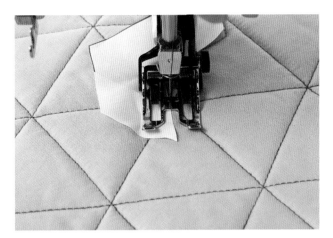

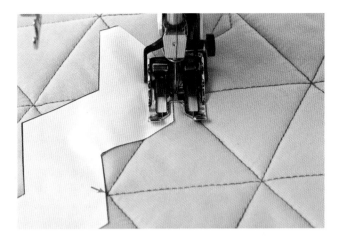

5. Using the edge of the template as a guide, stitch with the walking foot, pivoting with the needle down at the corners. Stitch to the last arrow on the template and stop with the needle down.

6. Raise the presser foot, carefully peel up the template, and move it forward (leapfrog-style). Place the first arrow next to the needle and align the remaining arrows at the intersections of stitch lines. Lower the presser foot.

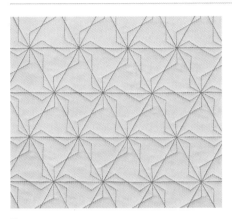

Note: As more quilting is done, the quilt will shrink up a little—I call this compaction. You may have to stretch the quilt or squish the template somewhat to get the template to fit as you go along. It is important that the arrows on the template be aligned with the intersections. After stitching the third set of "Z" curves, this pattern now looks like Whirling Stars (page 24), with points not curves, and the blades spin in the opposite direction.

7. Stitch "Z" curves over all the parallel lines in one direction, then over the next set of parallel lines, and then over the 3rd set. A "Z" is formed over each leg of each triangle.

This is a good quilting pattern as is, and you could stop here, but if you want to turn it into symmetrical six-pointed stars, keep going.

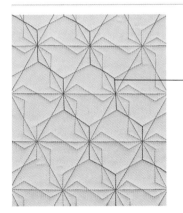

Overstitching on short center lines of stars

Note: You do not need the template for this step—use the lines and corners as guides. You will be stitching over previous stitching lines (overstitching) on the short center lines of the stars, so do your best to make the stitches match up. Perfection is not required, but you can work toward it.

8. Stitch mirror-image "Z" curves (shown in blue stitching in the photo) over all 3 sets of parallel lines. The overstitching goes through the spokes of the stars, then through the intersections that make the points of the stars, and then to the next corner of a spoke.

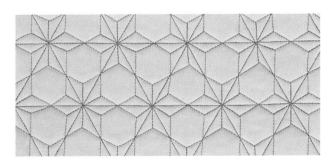

9. Continue to fill the area.

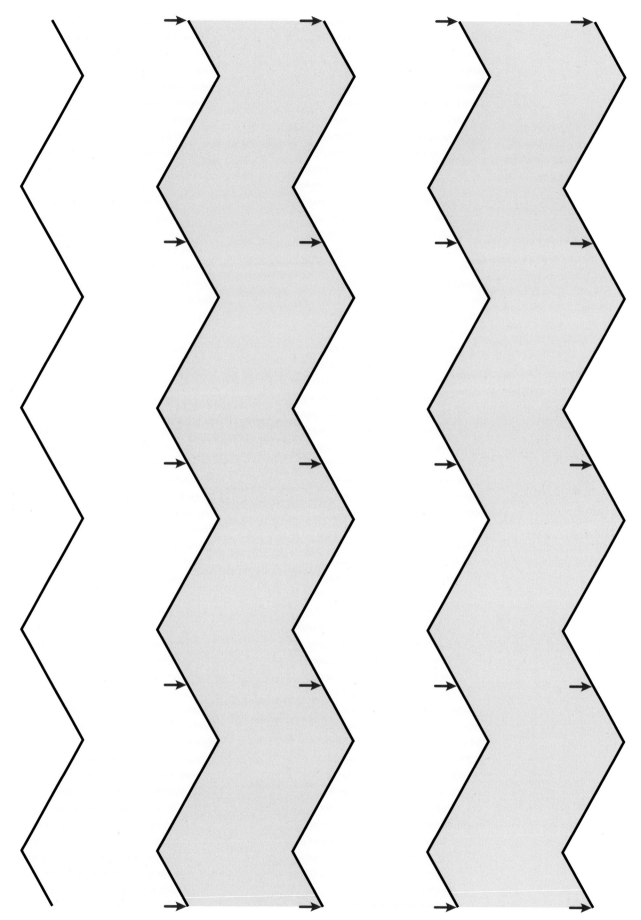

Six-Pointed Star template pattern

CHAPTER 4

Clamshell-Based Patterns

T he Clamshell pattern has a long tradition in the quilting world as a background fill design. The shape repetition is very basic—half circles placed end to end to create scallops, arranged in staggered rows.

This pattern looks best with the arc of the scallops pointing upward, toward the top of the quilt, although it can be used with the scallops pointing in other directions. To fill an area, start at the top of the area to be filled and stitch a complete row of half circles and then work downward.

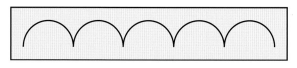

A complete row of scallops. If you want the scallops pointing in a different direction, place the first row accordingly.

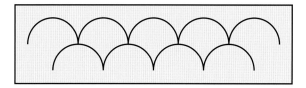

Staggered second row of half circles to make the clamshell pattern

Copy the template pattern (page 31) on sticky label paper, cut out the green template, and then trim it just above the red line. Peel off the paper backing. Position the template so the tops of the scallops are along a straight line of the space you want to fill. If the top of the area to be quilted is not a straight line, start lower down where you can complete a long row; then you can work upward to complete fragments of clamshells.

Note: Cut the template carefully to create a squared-off notch that will give you room to stitch the points of the clamshells. The actual stitching line is the black line of the template, which has been trimmed off. You will stitch next to the cut edge of the template, where the black line used to be.

Notes:

■ If you want to center the design in your quilt space, you can score 90° baselines (page 17) in the center of the space. Align the notches of the template along the horizontal score line and align a notch or the top of an arc on the vertical score line. Work outward from the center, stitching parallel rows of clamshells.

■ The stitching can be done with a walking foot. Having a knee lift for the presser foot (such as the Bernina Freehand System) really helps—you can use your knee to lift the presser foot to help you slowly stitch around the curve. If you feel confident, you can use free-motion stitching, the advantage of which is that the quilt doesn't have to be turned at all.

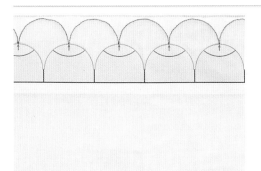

1. Stitch one row of scallops, leapfrogging the template from end to end to complete the 1st row. For the 2nd row, position the template so that the red arrows at the top of the template match the bottom of the 1st row of scallops. Stitch.

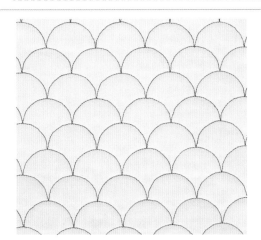

2. Repeat to fill the space with rows of clamshells.

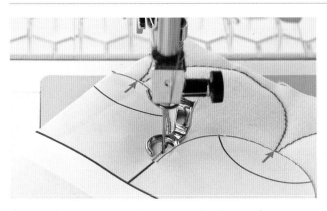

If the free-motion presser foot goes under the template, stop with the needle down and lift the presser foot back on top of the template.

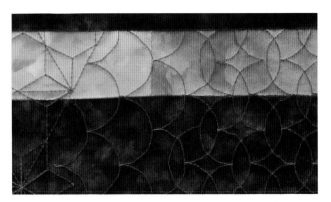

Detail of *Love at First Sight* by Kathy King

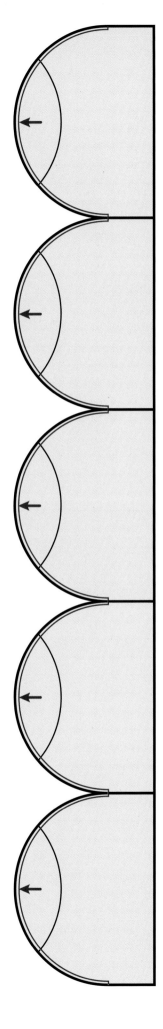
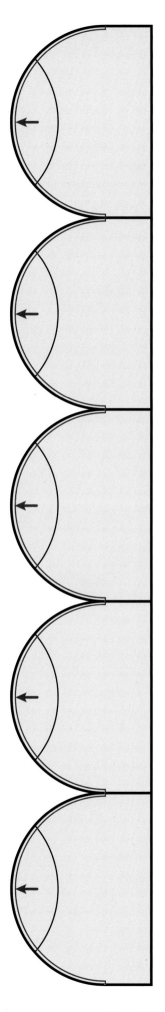
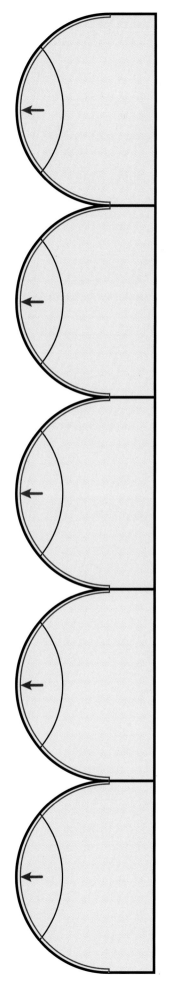
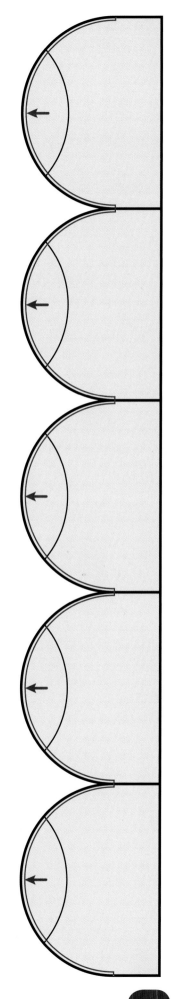

Clamshells template pattern   Clamshell-Based Patterns

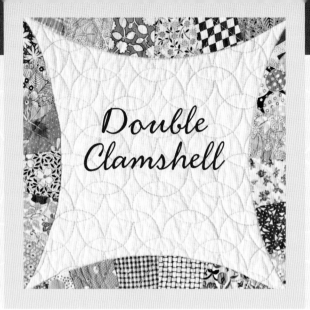

Double Clamshell

I found the Double Clamshell design while looking at a book on Japanese samurai and their armor. I saw it portrayed in only one centuries-old painting, and I haven't seen this exact pattern in any books I have read on Sashiko stitching patterns. This lovely pattern is simply two layers of clamshells placed one over the top of the other. The trick to doing this is in the placement, of course.

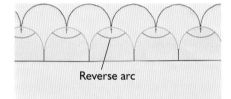

Reverse arc

1. Copy the template pattern (page 31) on sticky label paper, cut out the green template, and then trim it just above the red line. Peel off the paper backing. Position the template as desired in the area to be quilted. Stitch.

2. Fill the area with rows of simple scallops (page 29).

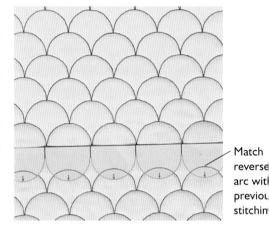

Match reverse arc with previous stitching

3. Starting at the bottom of the area to be filled, position the template to start the 2nd layer of reversed clamshells. The black arcs on the template should be aligned with the stitching.

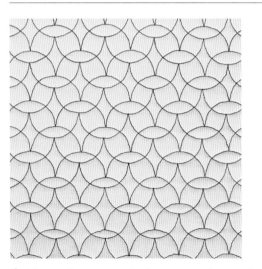

4. After each row is stitched, reposition the template, moving upward with the previously stitched layer of clamshells. Stagger alternating rows as with the 1st layer. Stitch row by row until the space is filled with the 2nd layer of clamshells.

Note: Because of compacting, the template may not fit as precisely as it should for the second layer of clamshells. You may need to stretch the quilt to make the template fit or squish the template curves a little closer together.

Kissing Clams

The Kissing Clams pattern has clamshells oriented in four different directions with the half circles "kissing" one another. It looks more complicated than the other patterns, but it is actually quite simple and can be done without marking by using a sticky template. The template consists of a series of opposing 1½"-diameter half circles.

This quilting design is a fun background fill with a lot of movement.

1. Determine a center point for starting. If symmetry is needed, the starting point should be in the center of the area to be quilted. With a dull tapestry needle, score horizontal and vertical lines at a 90° angle off the center point (page 7).

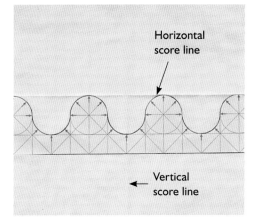

2. Copy the template pattern (page 35) on sticky label paper. Note that one rectangle makes 2 strips of templates after it is cut along the center curve. Peel off the backing paper and place the template with the tops of the half circles positioned along the horizontal score line and the green arrow on the vertical score line.

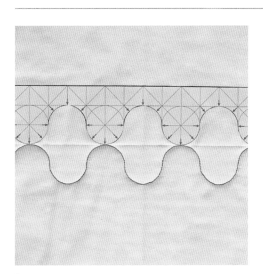

3. Stitch along the curved edge of the template. Then rotate the template 180° and place it on the other side of the horizontal score line, so that the tops of the half circles are touching the tops of the half circles from the previous row. Keep the green arrow on the vertical score line.

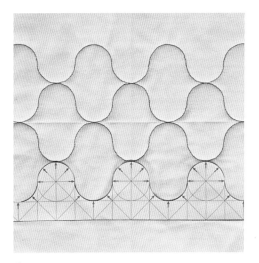

4. Continue stitching rows outward from the center, placing the template so the tops of the half circles touch one another.

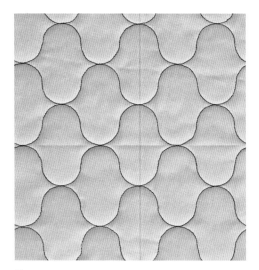

5. Fill the area with more horizontal rows. The pattern doesn't look like clamshells yet. Half the pattern is complete.

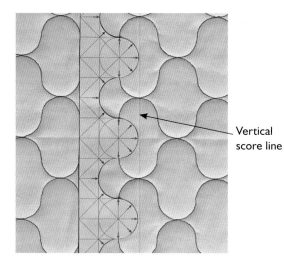

Vertical score line

6. Place the template with the tops of the half circles placed along the vertical score line and a green arrow on the horizontal score line with side green arrows matching previous stitching.

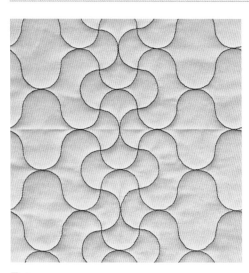

7. Stitch these vertical rows along the curved edge of the template, rotating the template in alternating rows as before. You will start to see the kissing clams as soon as the center rows are completed.

8. Continue to fill the area.

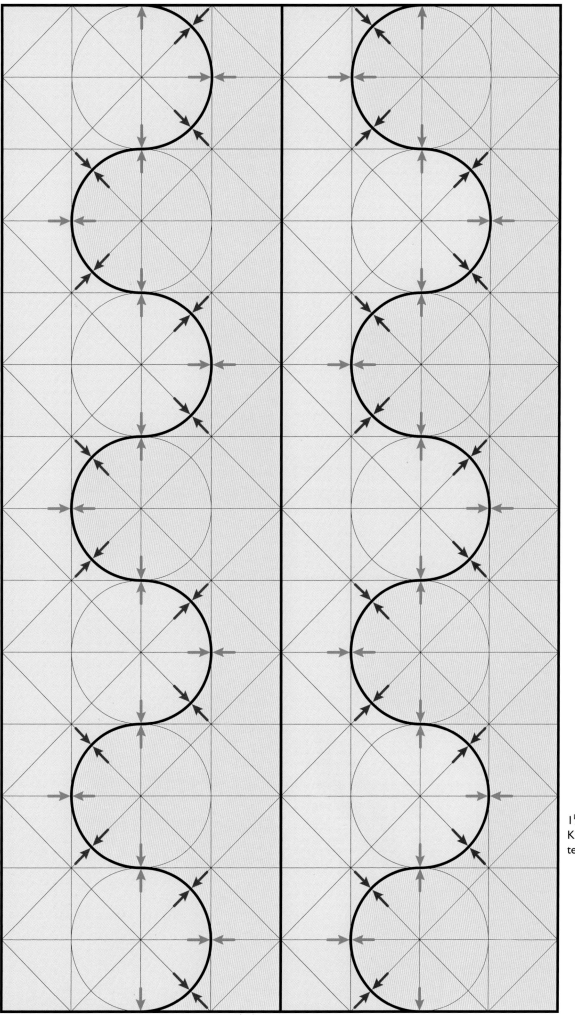

1½″ Circle and
Kissing Clams
template pattern

CHAPTER 5

Sinuous Geometric Curves

This chapter is a continuation of the previous chapter on clamshell-based patterns. After all, clamshells are made up of curves. The points of the clamshells help get the pattern lined up and correctly spaced. Other curved patterns may not necessarily have points and may thus seem more difficult to keep evenly spaced. However, there are tricks you can use to keep the curves consistently aligned.

Jigsaw

The Jigsaw pattern is a shape that reminds me of a jigsaw puzzle piece. The pattern uses the same type of template as was used to create the Kissing Clams pattern, but the diameter of the half circles for this pattern is ¾".

Copy the template pattern (page 38) on sticky label paper. Note that one rectangle makes two strips of templates after it is cut along the center curve. Peel off the paper backing. You will need two separate template strips to work this design. *For this pattern, the bottom of the template is the long straight edge.*

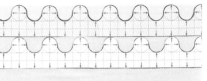

Straight edge

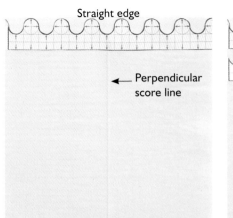

← Perpendicular score line

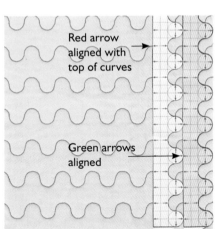

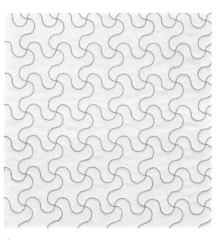

1. If you have a straight edge in the quilt area you need to fill, start the pattern on the straight edge. If you don't have a straight edge, score a line in the desired direction of the 1st set of curves. Score another line perpendicular (90°) to this line or to the straight edge. Place the tops of the curves of one of the templates against the straight edge or the score line. Have one outside green arrow (near the bottom of the template) on the perpendicular line. Stitch along the curved edge of the template.

2. Place the 2nd template so the inside green arrows at the top of the circles meet the green arrows on the bottom of the 1st template. Remove the 1st template. Stitch along the curved edge of this 2nd template.

3. Continue by alternating the 2 templates over each other and stitching until the area has been filled. Half the design is complete.

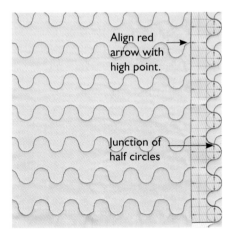

Align red arrow with high point.

Junction of half circles

Red arrow aligned with top of curves

Green arrows aligned

4. To stitch the set of perpendicular rows, position the template so that the red arrows on the bottom of the template are aligned with the highest stitched point of the half circles of the previous set of rows. One of the red arrows in each circle touches the junction of the 2 opposing half circles of the previous rows. Stitch along the curved edge of the template.

5. Place the 2nd template for the next row, lining up the straight edge 1st. The red arrows at the bottom of the 2nd template touch the tops of the curves of the previous layer. The inside green arrows at the top of the circles meet the green arrows on the bottom of the 1st template. Remove the 1st template; then stitch along the curved edge of the 2nd template.

6. Continue by alternating the 2 templates over each other and stitching until the area has been filled.

Note: The tops of the half circles may slightly overlap the 1st template because the quilting you have completed has compacted the quilt. Peel off the 1st template before stitching.

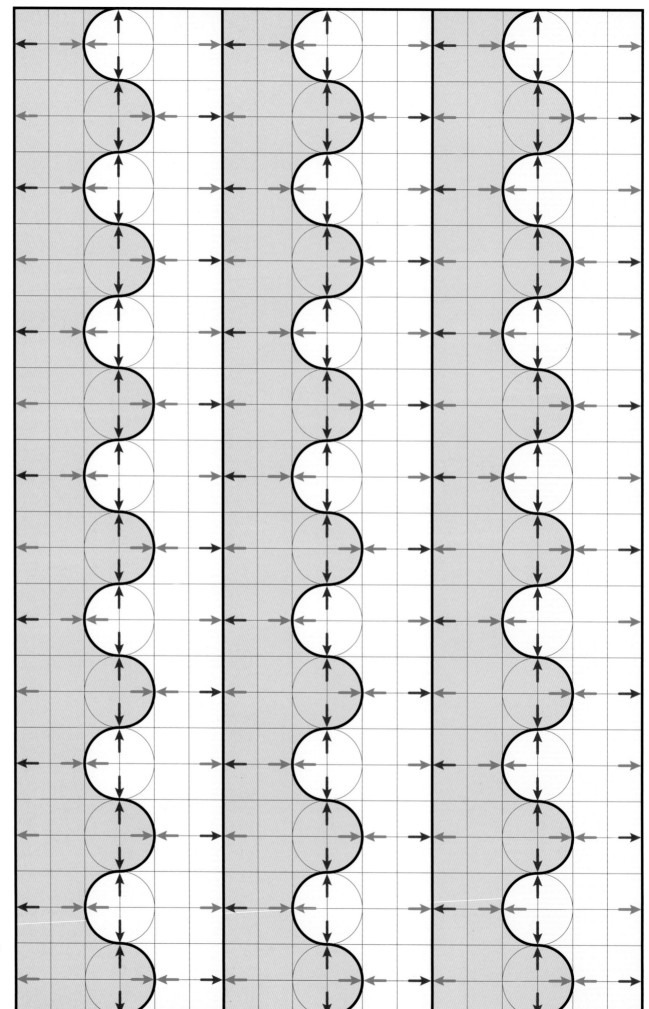

¾" Circle
Template

Jigsaw template
pattern

Trained Bubbles

Perfect circles seem like they would be hard to create. Mine are not as perfect as a computer would make them, but they are quite acceptable. I call this pattern Trained Bubbles because all the circles are a uniform size and are neatly in their places, row by row.

Copy the 1½″ circle template pattern (page 35) on sticky label paper. Note that one rectangle makes two strips of templates after it is cut along the center curve. Peel off the paper backing paper. *For this pattern, the bottom of the template is the long straight edge.*

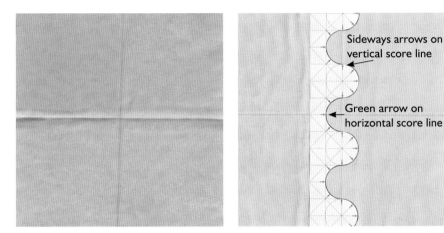

Sideways arrows on vertical score line

Green arrow on horizontal score line

I. Score 90° base lines (page 17).

2. Center the template by placing the sideways green arrows (located at the junctions of 2 opposing half circles) along the vertical score line. Place one of the outside green arrows at the bottom of a circle on the horizontal score line.

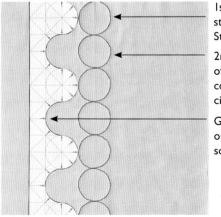

1st row of stitching in Step 2

2nd row of stitching completes circle shape

Green arrow on horizontal score line

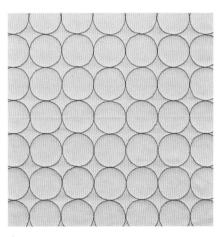

3. Stitch along the curved edge of the template. Rotate the template 180°. Again, line up the sideways green arrows along the vertical score line and place one of the outside green arrows at the bottom of a circle on the horizontal score line. Stitch along the curved edge of the template. This stitching line will complete the circle shape for a row of touching circles, or trained bubbles. Place the template next to the completed stitched circles so the inside green arrows at the tops of the curves just meet the previous line of stitching. One of the outside green arrows at the bottom of the template is on the horizontal score line.

4. Stitch along the curved edge of the template. Rotate the template 180° and line it up so that an outside green arrow at the bottom of a circle is on the horizontal score line. Also align the side green arrows with the previous line of stitching. (The stitching at the top of the previous row of circles can just barely be seen at the bottom green outside arrows of the template.) Stitch along the curved edge of the template to complete another row of circles. Repeat these rows of circles on either side of the center row until the area is filled.

Orange Peel

Create an allover pattern of trained bubbles (page 39) using the 1½"-diameter template (page 35) or the ¾"-diameter template (page 38); or reduce the size of the template on a photocopy machine or scanner and make a ½"-diameter template. Create the size needed to fill your quilting space. Continue with the following steps using the template you used for the trained bubbles.

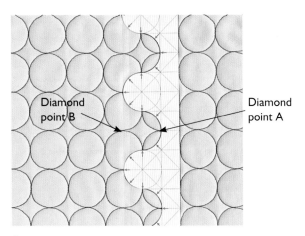

1. Place the template so that all the green arrows align with the points of the diamonds created between the circles. Stitch along the curved edge of the template.

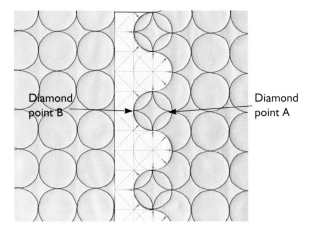

2. Rotate the template 180° and align the green arrows with the points of the diamond shape. (For placement, note the locations of Diamond point A and Diamond point B relative to the placement of the templates in both photographs for Steps 1 and 2.) Stitch along the curved edge of the template.

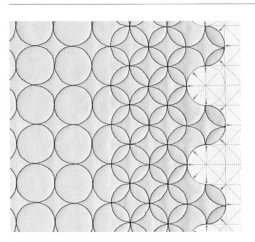

3. Continue stitching toward the edge of the quilt. Half of the quilt area is filled. (In the samples shown, the Orange Peel pattern started in the middle of the quilt area and progressed outward in one direction. Then the pattern was completed in the other direction.)

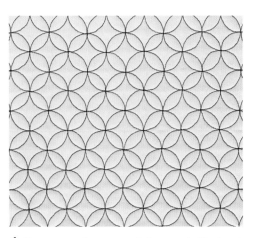

4. Repeat row by row until the area is filled and you have a gorgeous background pattern—easy to do but very impressive.

Curvy Links

Sometimes I have happy accidents. The following 2 patterns were created when I was trying much too hard to think up a template for the Orange Peel pattern (page 40).

Copy the 1½" circle template pattern (page 35) on sticky label paper. Note that one rectangle makes two strips of templates after it is cut along the center curve. Peel off the paper backing. *For this pattern, the bottom of the template is the long straight edge.*

1. Score 90° baselines (page 17).

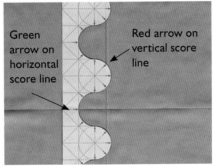

Green arrow on horizontal score line

Red arrow on vertical score line

2. Center the template by placing the inside 45° red arrows (near the tops of the curves) along the vertical score line and one outside green arrow (near the bottom of the template) on the horizontal score line. Stitch along the curved edge of the template.

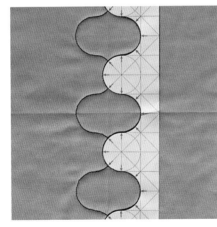

3. Rotate the template 180° and line up the inside 45° red arrows along the vertical score line and one outside green arrow (near the bottom of the template) with the horizontal score line. Stitch along the curved edge of the template. This completes one row of the pattern. A football-shaped area is created where the curves intersect.

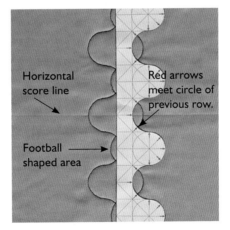

Horizontal score line

Red arrows meet circle of previous row.

Football shaped area

4. Rotate the template 180° and move it over so that the 45° red arrows on the outside of the circle (near the bottom of the template) meet the outside half circles of the previous row and the bottom of the template is on the points of the football shapes formed by the 1st row. Additionally, one of the outside green arrows of a circle (near the bottom of the template) should be on the horizontal score line. Stitch along the curved edge of the template.

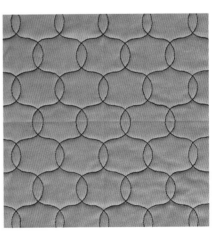

5. Rotate the template 180° and move it over so that the inside 45° red arrows (near the tops of the curves) touch the outside of the circles just stitched and one outside green arrow (near the bottom of the template) is aligned with the horizontal score line. Stitch. Continue stitching rows, rotating the template as you move out from the center until the area is filled.

Baseballs

Wouldn't the Baseballs pattern be great on a quilt for the sports fan? It is simply a continuation of the Curvy Links pattern.

Create an allover pattern of curvy links (page 41). *For this pattern, the bottom of the template is the long straight edge.*

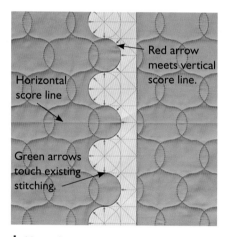

Red arrow meets vertical score line.

Horizontal score line

Green arrows touch existing stitching.

1. Using the same template as for the Curvy Links, center the template along the vertical score line so the outside red 45° arrows (near the bottom of the template) meet this score line, the green side arrows touch existing stitching from the 1st set of the Curvy Links rows, and one of the outside green circle arrows (near the bottom of the template) meets the horizontal score line. Stitch along the curved edge of the template.

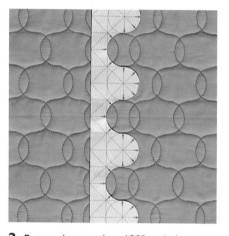

2. Rotate the template 180° and place it so the outside red 45° arrows (near the bottom of the template) meet the vertical score line, the green side arrows touch existing stitching from the 1st set of Curvy Links rows, and one of the outside green arrows (near the bottom of the template) meets the horizontal score line.

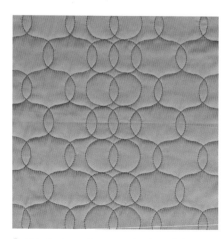

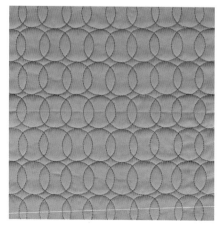

3. Stitch along the curved edge of the template.

4. Continue working rows out from the center until the area is filled. While working outward, keep the system of rotating the template for each successive row. Make sure that the green side arrows meet stitching from the 1st set of Curvy Links rows and keep one outside green circle arrow at the bottom of the template aligned with the horizontal score line.

Play with these half-circle templates on a sample quilt sandwich. You may come up with some happy accidents of your own. Some may work, some may not, but it can be fun just to experiment.

CHAPTER 6

Patterns with Pivot Points

OK, I lied. Some of these patterns will require a little marking. In this chapter I will keep it to the barest minimum—only tiny dots will be marked for pivot points on two of the quilting designs.

Pinwheels

Pinwheels is a fun and angular pattern with lots of movement. It's simple to stitch and can also be easily scaled up or down to suit your needs.

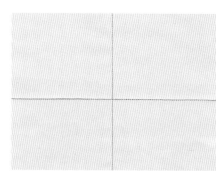

1. Determine a center point for starting. Score 90° baselines through the center point (page 17). Stitch these lines.

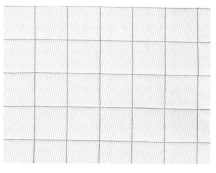

2. Create a 1½″ grid (page 17) of cross-hatching using your walking foot and a seam guide (page 7).

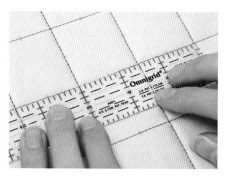

3. Measure (or eyeball) and mark tiny dots, using a removable marker, at the midpoint (¾″) on every side of every square.

Option: If you are truly confident, you can skip the marking and simply visualize the midpoint as you stitch.

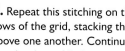 **Note:** Only half of these marks will actually be used, but I think it's easier to mark them all rather than taking the time to figure out which ones need to be marked.

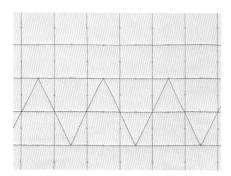

Midpoints marked—your marks don't need to be this dark.

4. Using 2 rows of the grid, start stitching a straight line at a midpoint mark, stitch through a grid intersection, and stop at the next midpoint mark with your needle down. Turn the quilt and stitch a straight line through the next intersection and then to the next midpoint. Repeat until a zigzag row is complete.

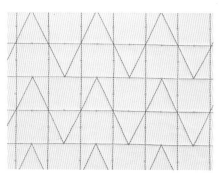

5. Repeat this stitching on the next 2 rows of the grid, stacking the points above one another. Continue until the area has been filled.

6. Rotate the quilt 90° and stitch the same zigzag pattern in 2 rows of grids, perpendicular to the 1st set of rows (shown in red in the photo). Start stitching at a midpoint of an empty grid square, stitch through the intersection where a horizontal row of zigzag has crossed, continue to the next midpoint, and stop with the needle down. Rotate the quilt and continue back through a grid intersection to the next midpoint. Repeat. Note that you stitch through the empty squares of the grid for this layer.

7. Fill the area.

Box Kites

The striking Box Kites pattern uses exactly the same rows of zigzag as Pinwheels (page 43); but there is no grid to place the lines for the zigzag, and the two layers of rows are slightly offset. How is this seemingly tricky pattern worked without marking and without a grid? The answer is by using masking tape guides.

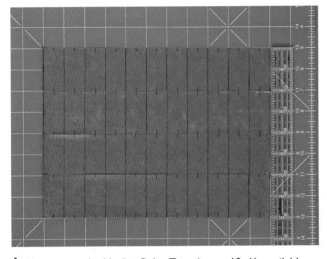

1. Use pre-marked Inchie Ruler Tape (pages 10, 11; available from C&T Publishing) or place 4 strips of 2″-wide masking tape (page 10) side by side along the horizontal grid lines of a cutting mat. The strips should be long enough to go across the quilt area you are filling. Place a ruler on one of the vertical lines on the cutting mat and draw a line with an ultrafine permanent marker across all the strips of tape. Mark vertical lines in 1″ increments across all the strips. Make short ½″ marks between the inch marks on the edges of all 4 strips; don't draw the ½″ marks all the way across the strips.

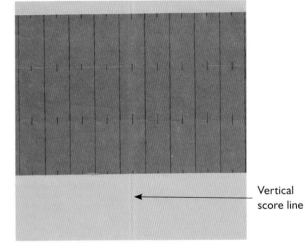

Vertical score line

2. Determine a center point for starting. Score 90° baselines through the center point (page 17). Place the edge of 1 strip of tape on the horizontal score line, matching one of the ½″ marks to the vertical score line. Place a strip of tape on each side of the 1st strip, aligning the marks.

Note: If you are quilting a large area, you may want to make many lengths of these masking tape guides at the same time to use as replacements when one no longer is sticky or has become tangled and unusable.

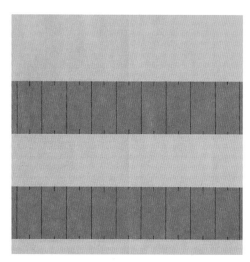

3. Remove the center strip of tape and set it aside carefully—you will use it again. The area between the tape strips is the area to be stitched.

4. Starting on one of the inch marks, stitch diagonally across to the inch mark that is 1″ farther down on the other strip. The walking foot may have an etched line on it right in front of the needle. Point this line directly at the inch mark you are sewing toward. Stop with the needle down and pivot. Then stitch to the inch mark that is 2″ down from where the stitching began.

5. Stitch across the space, pivoting and stitching to every other inch mark until the row is complete.

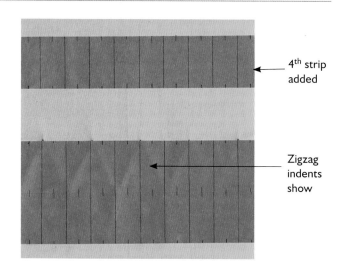

4th strip added

Zigzag indents show

6. Replace the center strip of tape over the stitching just completed, lining up the marks. Place the 4th strip of tape on the outer edge of 1 of the 2 outer strips. Remove the strip of tape that you placed the 4th strip next to and set it aside carefully—you will use it again. You can just barely see the points of the 1st row of stitching under the edge of the tape, and a zigzag indentation shows in the tape.

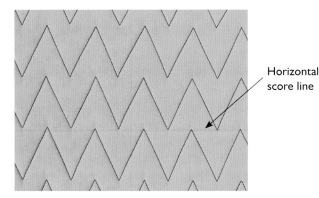

Horizontal score line

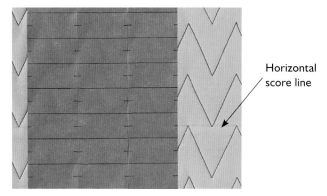

Horizontal score line

7. Stitch the next row of zigzag stitching, so the points are going in the same direction and are stacked right under the 1st row. Continue stitching rows in this manner until the area has been filled with zigzag.

8. To stitch the rows of zigzag in the opposite direction, place a strip of tape on the vertical score line matching one of the $1/2''$ marks to the horizontal score line. Place a strip of tape on each side of the 1st strip, aligning the marks.

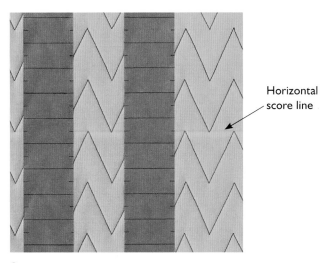

Horizontal score line

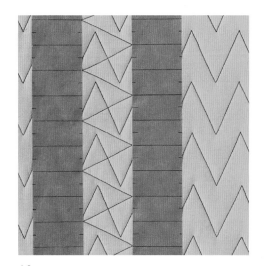

9. Remove the center strip of tape and set it aside carefully— you will use it again.

10. Stitch a row of zigzag as previously instructed, noting that the zigzag fits between the points of the previous rows and that the only place the new zigzag lines cross the previous stitching is in the middle of the row.

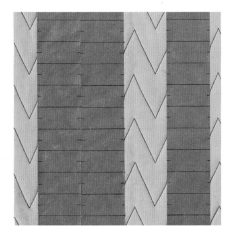

11. Align and replace the tape over the top of this row of stitching. The stitching that has already been done may have compacted the quilt slightly. To compensate for this, overlap the tape strips slightly—by about $1/16''$. Continue moving outward from the center, and place the 4th strip of tape on the outer edge of one of the existing 3 strips of tape. Remove the tape strip between the 4th strip and the previous row of stitching to reveal the next area for stitching. The $1/2''$ marks should be lying on (or at least be close to) the 1st set of zigzag stitching lines, and the 1″ marks should align with the points of the previous row.

12. Continue stitching rows until the area is filled and the pattern is complete.

Facets

With sparkle and appeal, Facets is another pattern that is easy to stitch with the help of masking tape guides. It also calls for stitching over previously stitched lines, or overstitching.

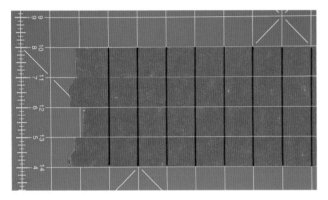

Note: If you are quilting a large area, you may want to make many lengths of these masking tape guides at the same time to use as replacements when one no longer is sticky or has become tangled and unusable.

1. Use pre-marked Inchie Ruler Tape (pages 10, 11; available from C&T Publishing) or place 4 strips of 1″-wide masking tape (page 10) side by side along the horizontal grid lines of a cutting mat. The strips should be long enough to go diagonally across the quilt area you are filling. Place a ruler on one of the vertical lines on the cutting mat and draw a line with an ultrafine permanent marker across all the strips of tape. Mark vertical lines in 1″ increments across all the strips.

2. Determine a center point for starting the quilting pattern. Score diagonal 90° baselines through the center point (page 17).

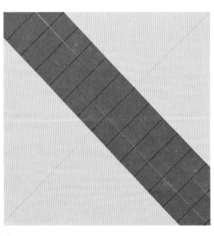

3. Place the edge of 1 strip of tape along a score line, matching one of the 1″ marks with the 2nd score line. Place a strip of tape on each side of the 1st strip, aligning the marks.

4. Remove the center strip, revealing the area to be stitched.

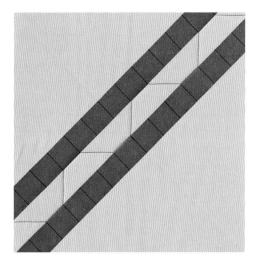

5. Beginning at the topmost inch mark on the right-hand strip of tape, stitch diagonally across to the inch mark that is 1″ farther down on the other strip. The walking foot may have an etched line on it right in front of the needle. Point this line directly at the diagonal inch mark. Stop with the needle down and pivot. Then stitch along the edge of the tape to the next inch mark and stop with the needle down. Pivot and stitch diagonally between the 2 strips of tape to what would be the 3rd corresponding 1″ mark on the right-hand strip of tape. Then stitch down the edge of this tape to the next 1″ mark and pivot.

6. Continue stitching from side to side between the tape strips until the row is complete.

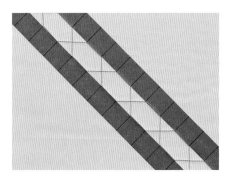

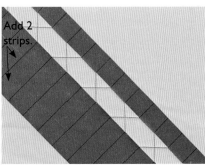

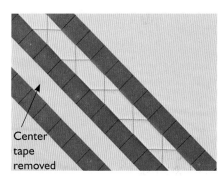

7. Start from the opposite side and stitch a line that is the mirror image of the 1st line of stitching. Follow the same pattern: straight, diagonal, straight, diagonal, and so on.

8. Do not remove any tape yet. Align and place the other 2 tape strips on the outer edge of 1 of the strips that is already in place. Be sure to keep the 1″ marks continuous across the strips.

9. Remove the center strip of tape of the 3 strips that are next to each other and set it aside carefully—you will use it again.

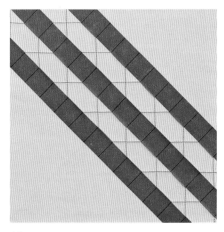

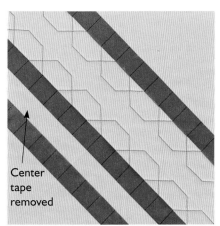

10. Make 2 more mirror-image lines of stitching to create a row in this space. Note that the stitching lines between the tape strips combine to form an overall grid pattern.

11. Align and place the other 2 tape strips on the outer edge of 1 of the strips that is already in place. Remove the center strip and stitch 2 more mirror-image lines of stitching.

12. Continue in this manner until the area has been filled.

Now it is time to do a 2nd layer of the rows of stitching using the same pattern; however, this layer of rows will run perpendicular to the 1st layer. The tape guides will not be needed to accomplish this. All the necessary pivot points have been put in place by the previous stitching. This layer is where overstitching is required. The overstitching will be done on the pointed ends of the hexagons where a cross has formed. Start on one of these segments of lines and continue with the following steps.

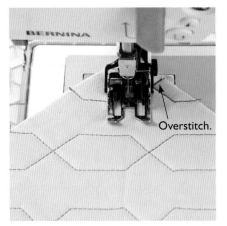

13. Starting at one corner, stitch over the 1st line of stitching as shown. Stop at the corner with the needle down and pivot.

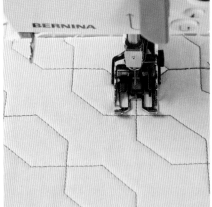

14. Overstitch across to the nearest corner of the next row. Pivot.

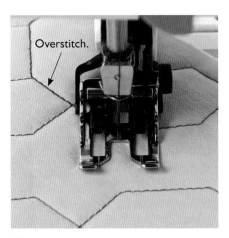

15. Overstitch the length of the diagonal line to the next corner, pivot, and aim at the next adjacent corner of the next row.

16. Proceed down the row as for the 1st layer of stitching (shown in red in the photo). Stitch a mirror image of this row (also shown in red). One perpendicular row of the 2nd layer of stitching is complete.

17. Complete the rest of the rows to fill the space.

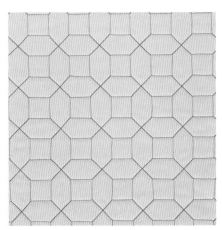

Notice that if the design is turned 45° so that the score lines are horizontal and vertical, the pattern has a slightly different look.

Zoids

I like to get cute with names sometimes, but "tessellating trapezoids" is just too much of a tongue twister. Three trapezoids in a triangle look like a Zoid to me. I saw this pattern worked out in paving bricks at a building in my city and had to try it out for a quilting pattern.

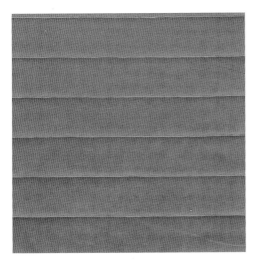

1. Score a horizontal line (page 17) and stitch on that line. Using a walking foot and a seam guide set at $1\frac{1}{2}$″ (page 7), stitch a set of parallel lines. Fill the space.

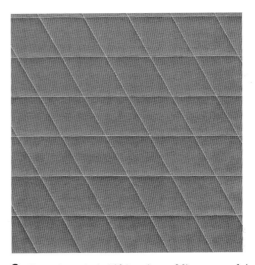

2. Place the ruler's 60° line (page 20) on one of the 1st set of stitched lines and score a line along the edge of the ruler. Stitch on this line. Set the seam guide at $1\frac{1}{2}$″ and, using a walking foot, stitch a 2nd set of parallel lines over the first. Fill the space.

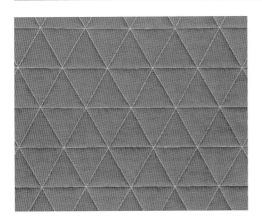

3. Stitch straight lines across the shorter diameters of the diamond shapes, connecting the intersections of the grid lines you just stitched. Fill the space. Create a $1\frac{1}{2}$″ equilateral triangular grid.

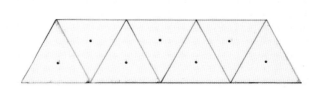

4. Trace the Triangle template (page 52) onto template plastic. Make holes at the dots, exactly $\frac{1}{2}$″ from all sides of the triangle, using a tiny hole punch or an awl.

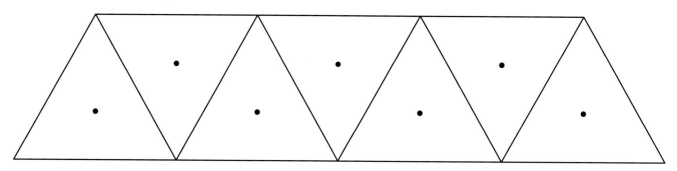

Triangle template with center dots

5. Place the template plastic over the stitched triangular grid, matching the lines of the triangles. Make a small dot in the middle of each triangle through the hole in the template, using a fine pencil or other removable marker.

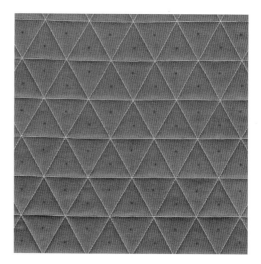

All triangles have a dot in the center.

Note: To complete the trapezoids, you will need to stitch $1/2''$ from the edges of the triangles. If the distance from the needle to the edge of your walking foot is $1/2''$, you don't need to use a seam guide. If this distance is not $1/2''$, use a seam guide (page 7).

A trapezoid has 2 parallel and 2 nonparallel sides. The parallel sides of the trapezoids will be stitched using the $1/2''$ guide. All the remaining lines will be stitched or overstitched parallel to one of the sides of the triangles.

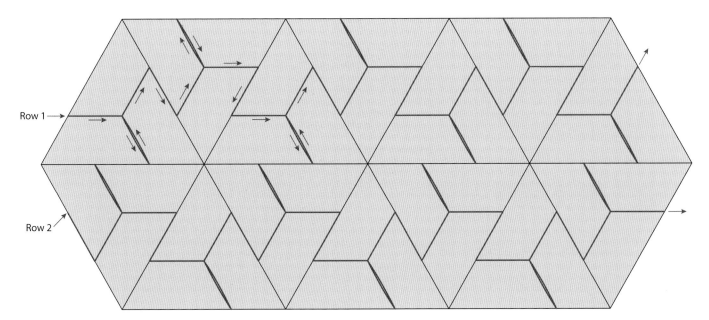

Row 1 →

Row 2 →

6. The red lines show the path of the stitching that creates the trapezoids. The double lines indicate overstitching. Start at the arrow on the top row on the left. Stitch the 1st segment of the line parallel to the base of the triangle, stop with the needle down, and pivot. Stitch to the baseline while parallel to the right side of the triangle, stop with the needle down, and pivot. Overstitch the segment just stitched, stop at the center dot with the needle down, and pivot. Stitch to the right side of the triangle parallel to the left side of the triangle, stop with the needle down, and pivot. Overstitch down the right side of the triangle to within $1/2''$ of the next triangle (so that when you pivot and turn into the next triangle you are parallel to its right side). Stop with the needle down and pivot. Work the next triangle in much the same way, with the segment of overstitching going directly opposite.

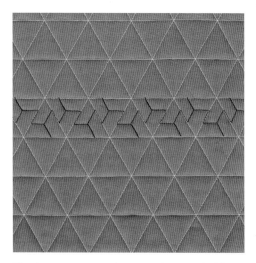

The basic pattern is shown in this sample. You can see how the path flows through the row (shown in blue in the photo.)

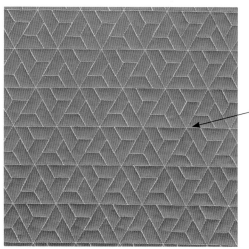

Center of 6 fan blades

7. Continue stitching to fill the area. The trapezoids look like 6 rotating fan blades when done correctly

If this stitching path is followed for one row and then a mirror image is used for the next row, a different pattern emerges. The trapezoids look like maple leaves. It's not a mistake if that's the desired look, but consistency is needed to maintain the pattern.

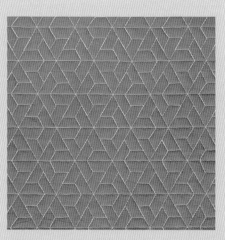

Zoids—Maple Leaf

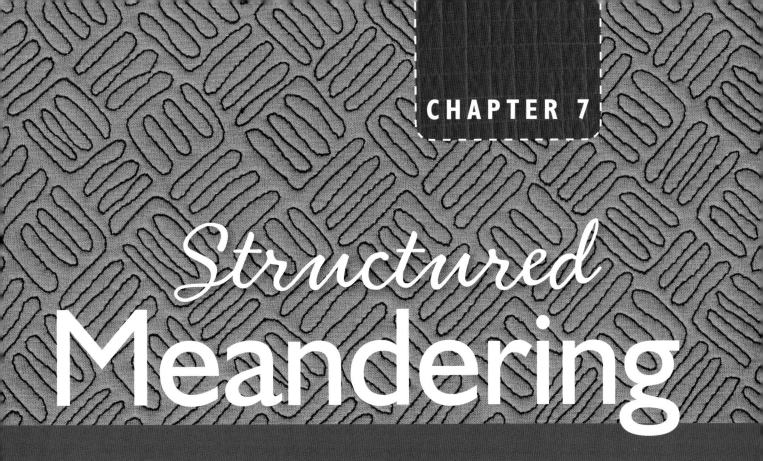

CHAPTER 7

Structured Meandering

Having judged several prestigious quilt shows, I find that I (and many of my fellow judges) look on machine-quilted meandering, which some call stippling, as less than interesting. However, the addition of some structure makes meandering look more impressive, adds excitement and texture, and makes a pleasing background fill.

Doodle Weave

The Doodle Weave pattern, the simplest structured meander, is based on a square. Each square is filled with a back and forth stitching line that has 4 or 6 turns and then a 5th or 7th turn to take the line to the adjacent square. This pattern is repeated until a row of squares has been filled working from top to bottom. Then the next row is stitched from bottom to top. You will need to look ahead to the last square of the row to see where the line of stitching is going to end up. If it will end up on the opposite corner needed to start the next row, you will need to stitch six lines rather than five and space the lines in that square accordingly.

The lines and turns do not need to be particularly smooth or even. The juxtapositions and counterpoints of the squares create a lovely woven texture.

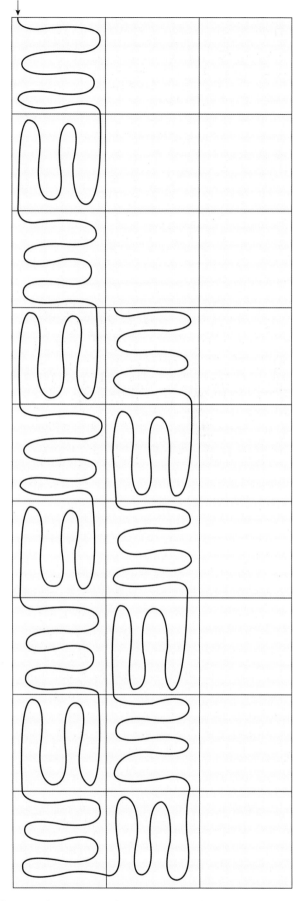

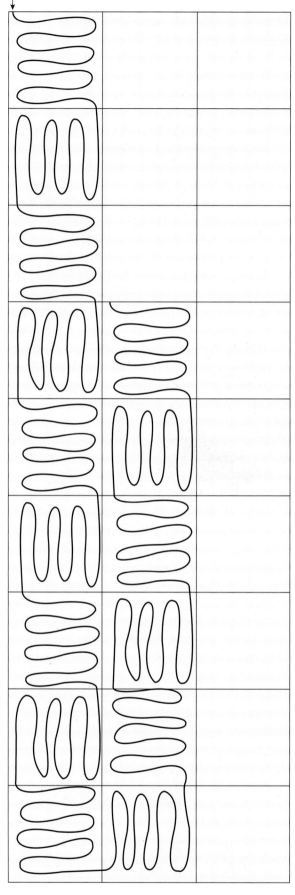

Practice this pattern with paper and pencil to get the rhythm. Place a piece of tracing paper over the 1″ grid and trace along the path of the doodle. Continue into the blank squares until you have filled the grid. A half page of grid should suffice. The grid can be slightly smaller than 1″ if needed.

If denser quilting is desired, expand the Doodle Weave pattern to seven lines per square. I find this condensed version to be more to my taste. Trace this one on the grid provided.

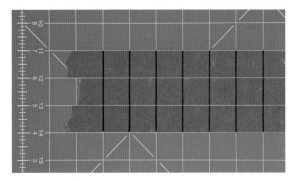

1. Use pre-marked Inchie Ruler Tape (pages 10, 11; available from C&T Publishing) or place 3 strips of 1″-wide masking tape (page 10) side by side along the horizontal grid lines of a cutting mat. The strips should be long enough to go across the quilt area you are filling. Place a ruler on one of the vertical lines on the cutting mat and draw a line with an ultrafine permanent marker across all the strips of tape. Mark vertical lines in 1″ increments across all the strips.

Note: If you are quilting a large area, you may want to make many lengths of these masking tape guides at the same time to use as replacements when one no longer is sticky or has become tangled and unusable.

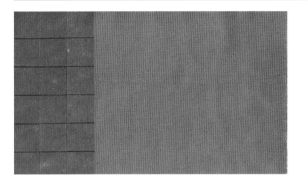

2. Place 3 strips of tape side by side on the quilt, aligning the inch marks. The rows can be stitched from one side of your quilt area to the other, or from the center out. A ruler may be used to set a straight line if needed.

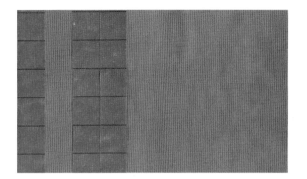

3. Remove the center strip of tape and place it along the right side of the right-hand strip of tape.

Note: If you want the Doodle Weave pattern to look precise, you will need to pay attention to the space that is to be filled. If the space is straight and rectangular, you may need to make sure that you place the tape parallel to the sides of your rectangle. This pattern was used on the royal blue areas of *Starcrossed* (page 16), and the space is rectangular on three sides. When quilting, I made sure that the tape was parallel to the black areas and that whole rows fit from side to side so that I didn't end up with a fraction of the pattern on the last row.

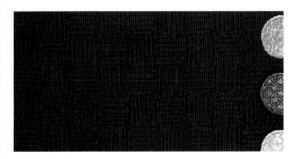

Note: If you look at the lines on the remaining strips of tape on your quilt area, you can see that they create boundaries for the 1″ squares on the strip of fabric that was revealed when the center strip of tape was removed. If you have trouble visualizing the squares, you can put a small piece of tape at the bottom and top of each square; however, the pieces will have to be removed as you stitch, and this interrupts the flow of the quilting.

4. Use a quilting or darning foot (consider a Bernina Stitch Regulator) and drop the feed dogs. If you have a needle-down option, set your machine for this. Start in the upper left corner of the top square, stitch 5 (or 7) lines horizontally and then travel to the square below and stitch 5 (or 7) lines vertically. Continue to the bottom of the row and stop in the lower right corner of the bottom square with your needle down.

5. Remove the center strip of tape and place it on the right side of the right-hand strip of tape, to reveal a new strip of fabric for stitching.

6. Stitch this row of squares from bottom to top using lines that are perpendicular to the lines in the corresponding squares to the left.

7. Continue by moving the tape row by row until the space is filled.

DIAGONAL OPTION

If you master the flow of the Doodle Weave pattern and do not require precision, the pattern can be done without guides. This works particularly well if the overall pattern is done on the diagonal. Keeping the inch square in mind, approximate the horizontal lines that fall within it, make the turn, and stitch the vertical lines below it. Work a row across the quilting space and then work rows back and forth until the space is filled. This pattern is complicated enough that any imprecision will not be noticed; even when done imperfectly, the pattern still makes an impressive filler design.

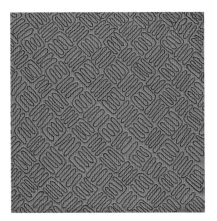

Structured meandering stitched on the diagonal without a grid

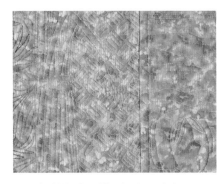

Detail of *We Give Thanks*; I used the diagonal Doodle Weave design to quilt the beige background.

Slanted Doodle Weave

You can also work Doodle Weave (page 55) with a diagonal slant by drawing the inch marks on the masking tape at a 60° or 45° angle to create diamonds.

Slanted Doodle Weave is a bit more challenging because the diamonds are harder to visualize than the squares, and maintaining the proper slant can be difficult. But with concentration, it can make a wonderful background fill.

1. Use Inchie Ruler Tape (pages 10, 11; available from C&T Publishing) or place at least 3 strips of 1″-wide masking tape (page 10) side by side along the horizontal grid lines of a cutting mat. The strips should be long enough to go across the quilt area you are filling. Place the 60° line of a large ruler along the edge of one strip of Inchie Ruler Tape or masking tape and use the edge of the ruler to draw a line across all the strips of tape.

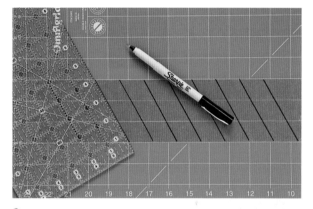

2. Use the 1″ line on the ruler to make a series of lines parallel to the line you have just drawn along the entire length of all the strips of tape.

Note: If you are quilting a large area, may want to make many lengths of these masking tape guides at the same time to use as replacements when one no longer is sticky or has become tangled and unusable.

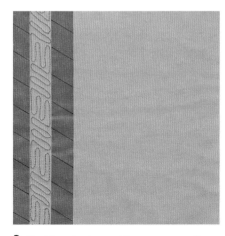

3. Position the tape strips on your quilt as described on pages 57-58, removing the center strip to create a 1″ wide space. Stitch diagonal lines in the 1st diamond and stitch opposing diagonals in every other diamond.

4. Continue to fill the area.

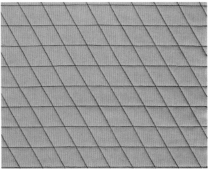

Triangle Doodle Weave

The Doodle Weave design can also be stitched inside equilateral triangles (page 21). The unquilted triangles create a lovely relief broken by the interesting texture of the doodled triangles.

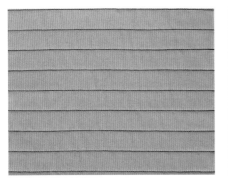

1. Score a horizontal line (page 17) and stitch on that line. Set the seam guide of your walking foot at 1″ (page 7) and stitch a set of parallel lines. Fill the space.

2. Place the ruler's 60° line (page 20) on one of the 1st set of stitched lines and score a line along the edge of the rule using a dull tapestry needle. Using the score line and the seam guide set at 1″, stitch a 2nd set of parallel lines over the 1st. Fill the space.

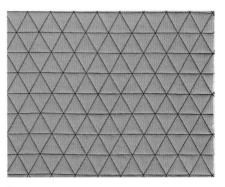

3. Stitch a straight line from one intersection to the next intersection to complete the 3rd set of parallel lines. Fill the space. You can still use the seam guide, but it is more important to be sure the new line of stitching goes right through the center of the previously stitched intersections. A triangular grid is formed.

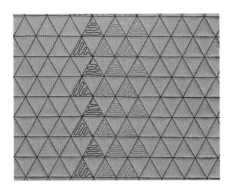

4. Change to a free-motion foot or a quilting foot and drop the feed dogs. Beginning at the top, stitch parallel to the left side and doodle back and forth until you reach the right corner; then drop to the next triangle that is sitting on its base directly below this corner. Doodle back

and forth horizontally until you reach the bottom left corner; then drop into the next triangle that is sitting on its base directly below this corner. Stitch parallel to the left side of the triangle and repeat until you have completed a staggered vertical row (in red). For the next row, continue in reverse order until you reach the top (in green). Every other triangle will be empty.

Note: Look for triangles that are sitting on their bases with their points upward as the quilt is facing you.

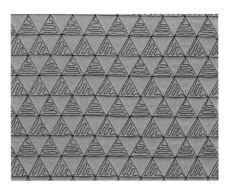

5. Continue to fill the triangles.

Hex Doodle Weave

The Hex Doodle Weave is a complicated doodle that requires a lot of concentration but looks absolutely fabulous. It can be worked with one color of thread all over, with one color for the grid and another for the doodle, or with a different color for each row of doodles. The pattern is created by six equilateral triangles that form a hexagon, along with an additional two triangles for traveling to the next hexagonal group.

This pattern could also be used for a wondrous effect in a Tumbling Blocks quilt. Most of the grid is already in place; just divide the 60° diamonds in half and complete the doodle over a block.

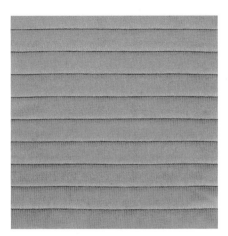

1. Score a horizontal line (page 17) and stitch on that line. Set the seam guide of your walking foot at 1″ (page 7) and stitch a set of parallel lines. Fill the space.

2. Place the ruler's 60° line (page 20) on one of the 1st set of stitched lines and score a line along the edge of the ruler using a dull tapestry needle. Using the score line and the seam guide set at 1″, stitch a 2nd set of parallel lines over the 1st. Fill the space.

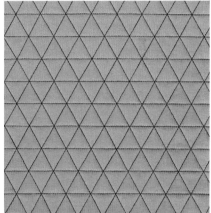

3. Stitch a straight line from one intersection to the next intersection. Fill the space. You can still use the seam guide, but it is more important to be sure the new line of stitching goes right through the center of the previously stitched intersections. A triangular grid is formed.

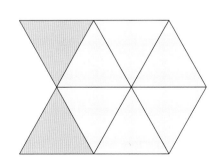

4. Choose 6 triangles that form a hexagon. Think of the hexagon as a pie made up of 6 triangular wedges, illustrated in blue, that converge at the center. The 2 traveling triangles are illustrated in pink.

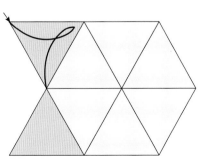

5. Change to a quilting foot or free-motion foot and drop the feed dogs. The blue and pink triangles make up a unit. Stitch a pointed loop in the traveling triangle as illustrated.

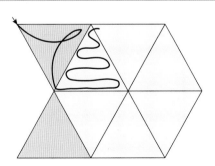

6. Stitch into the 1st wedge of the hexagon, paralleling the lower side of the triangle; fill up the wedge with an odd number of back and forth lines (5 or 7).

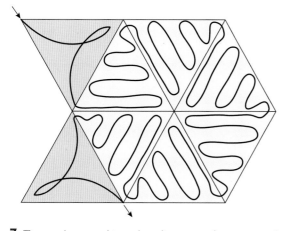

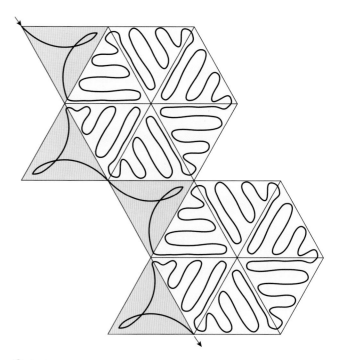

7. Turn and proceed into the adjacent wedge, once again working parallel to the side. Fill each of the wedges in this manner until you are back to the corner of the 1st traveling triangle. Then make another pointed loop in the next traveling triangle that points in the opposite direction.

8. Make another pointed loop in the next traveling triangle that points in the opposite direction and continue stitching the hexagons in diagonal rows.

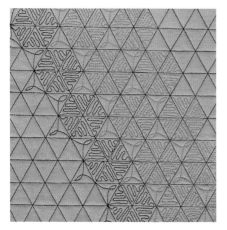

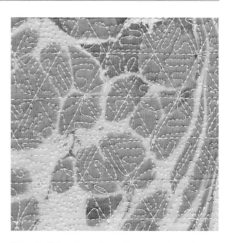

9. Work the units end to end to form a row of stitching that has the traveling loops on one side and the hexagons making up the bulk of the pattern on the other. The rows are side by side, and all the triangles have quilting once the pattern is done. The 1st row is shown in red, the 2nd in green, and the 3rd in orange.

10. Continue to fill the area

Detail of *Anodyne*. I used a gray thread to mute the vivid marbling of the background. I used a 1/2″ Equilateral Triangular Grid for the Hex Doodle Weave design. I found that the smaller the scale, the harder it is to get a perfect grid. However, the doodle quilting hides any inaccuracies in the grid.

CHAPTER 8

Gallery

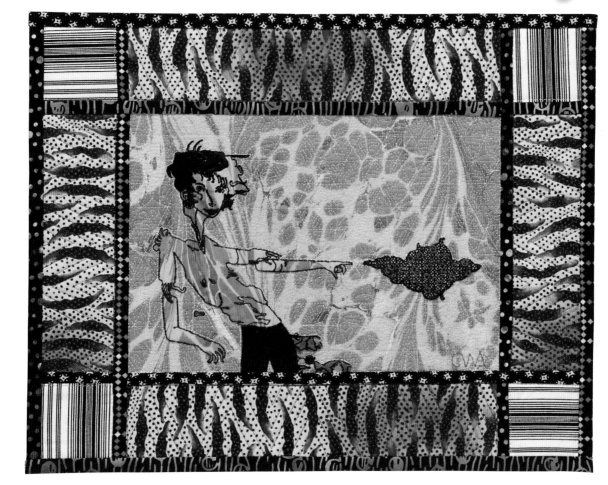

Anodyne by Charlotte Warr Andersen. The embroidery was based on a drawing by Davyn Peder Andersen. The Hex Doodle was used behind the figure to fill the background and bring out the figure.

We Give Thanks by Charlotte Warr Andersen. Available as a pattern from JWD Publishing, this quilt is an updated and simplified version of a quilt that Charlotte made in 1987.

Starcrossed by Charlotte Warr Andersen and Aubry Kae Andersen. This quilt was the inspiration for the development of the "One Line at a Time" approach and was a Best of Show winner at the Mid-Atlantic Quilt Festival. It is based on a design created by Charlotte's daughter, Aubry. Aubry did the painting for the faces and the warrior's body; Charlotte did the sewing, digitized embroidery, and quilting.

Finding My Way Back to Awasi by Robyn Moriarty Kruppa. Robyn has effectively used the Zoids pattern, as well as other patterns, in this lovely, tranquil quilt.

Love at First Sight by Kathy King. Kathy reduced some of the patterns in scale to make this wonderful quilt.

Set Me Free by Suzanne Hyland. This lively wall quilt was begun in a workshop Suzanne took with Judith Traeger. She has used the Kissing Clams pattern in the background.

(Yellow) Tang-o in Paradise by Lisa Brothman has wavering lines of the Doodle Weave that give the perfect texture to this underwater scene.

Frolicking Worms by Jan Tolman. Jan has used the Doodle Weave, Doodled Triangles, Clamshells, and Box Kites on this colorful little wallhanging.

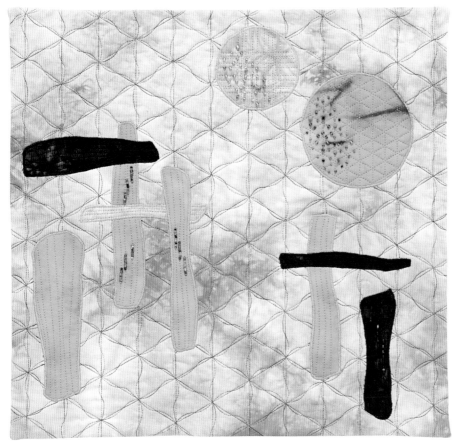

This funky little quilt, *Pagoda Moons*, by Beverly Hart features the Plaid pattern, Equilateral Triangles, and Whirling Stars.

Only partially completing the equilateral triangular grid and using half of the 6-Pointed Star pattern enhances the solar theme of *Daystar* by Jalaine Taylor. Jalaine has also used a pointed version of the Doodle Weave.

The simple quilting shapes used on *Steeplechase* complement rather than complicate the rich surface of this scrap quilt entirely made of reproduction fabrics.

Steeplechase by Jeana Kimball, quilted by Charlotte Warr Andersen using the Trained Bubbles and Facets patterns

Sunflowers by Georgia Bonesteel. This quilt is a re-creation of Marie Webster's *Sunflower* quilt. The original had hand quilted spider webs in the center, but Georgia decided to use the plaid pattern, carrying the straight lines out across the flowers.

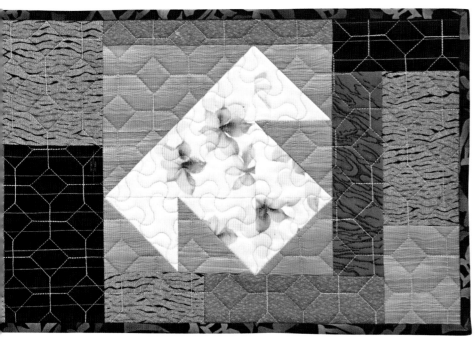

Dancing Kimonos is a table runner by Kathryn King. She has used the Facets pattern on the background and Jigsaw for the kimonos.

Galatea Adorned, a quilted garment by Charlotte Warr Andersen, was made for the 2008 Bernina Fashion Show. Photo by Kim Coffman, courtesy of Quilts, Inc.

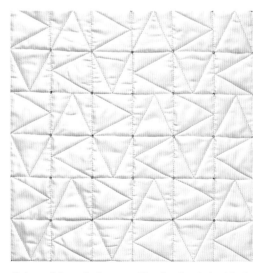

Galatea Adorned, close-up. Pinwheels stitched in 4 colors of thread on silk satin are embellished at each intersection of the grid with Swarovski® Hot-fix Crystals in 3 colors.

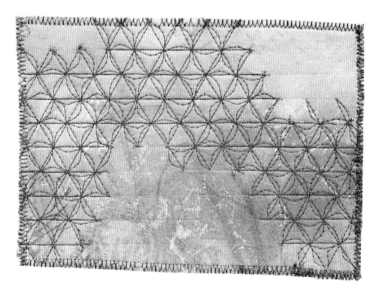

Jan Tolman miniaturized the Whirling Stars pattern and used a wonderful hand-dyed fabric to create this postcard-sized piece. Notice that Jan mixed S-curves and Z-curves for an interesting variation.

About the Author

Charlotte Warr Andersen is an avid and well-known quilter. She is a native of Salt Lake City, Utah. She learned many needle skills from her mother, but most of her quilting skills were self-taught or acquired by good observation. She lives with her husband, Eskild, two of her four children, and three dogs, Scruffy, Hugo, and Legion.

Most known for her pictorial quilts, Charlotte has authored two previous books: *Faces & Places—Images in Appliqué* and *Focus on Features—Life-like Portraits in Appliqué*. Unfortunately, these books are both out of print. Stitching a portrait is still her favorite pastime.

Charlotte travels to teach her stitching and quilting methods. Currently, she is serving as the president of the International Quilt Association.

Bibliography

Gaudynski, Diane, *Gaudynski's Machine Quilting Guidebook: Quilt Savvy,* American Quilter's Society: Paducah, Kentucky, 2006

Gaudynski, Diane, *Guide to Machine Quilting,* American Quilter's Society: Paducah, Kentucky, 2002

Parker, Mary, *Sashiko: Easy & Elegant Designs for Decorative Machine Embroidery,* Lark Books: Asheville, North Carolina, 1999

Roberts, Luise, *1000 Great Quilting Designs,* Reader's Digest: Pleasantville, New York, 2004

For more fine books and products such as Inchie Ruler Tape from C&T Publishing, ask for a free catalog:
C&T Publishing, Inc. P.O. Box 1456 | Lafayette, CA 94549
(800) 284-1114
Email: ctinfo@ctpub.com | Website: www.ctpub.com

C&T Publishing's professional photography services are now available to the public. Visit us at www.ctmediaservices.com.

For quilting supplies:
Cotton Patch 1025 Brown Ave. | Lafayette, CA 94549
Store: (925) 284-1177 | Mail order: (925) 283-7883
Email: CottonPa@aol.com | Website: www.quiltusa.com